Collins *gem*

DIGITAL Photography

Practical Tips for Great Digital Photographs

Patrick

G000152241

First published in 2005 by Collins, an imprint of HarperCollins*Publishers*
77–85 Fulham Palace Road, Hammersmith, London W6 8JB
everything clicks: www.collins.co.uk

Photography, text and design © HarperCollins *Publishers* Limited, 2005

Based on material from *Collins Need to Know? Digital Photography*

Created by: **Focus Publishing**, Sevenoaks, Kent
Project editor: Guy Croton
Editor: Vanessa Townsend
Designer: David Etherington
Project co-ordinator: Caroline Watson

The majority of photographs in this book were taken by the author.
For a detailed breakdown of photographic credits, see page 192.

A catalogue record for this book is available from the British Library

ISBN 0 00 719431 5

Colour reproduction by Digital Imaging
Printed and bound by Amadeus S.r.l., Italy

CONTENTS

GETTING STARTED

This tour of digital photography begins with the basics, and addresses many questions commonly asked by those new to the subject.

EVERYONE WANTS INSTANT COMMUNICATION

The internet has revolutionized communication. People can send and receive text and images on a daily, if not hourly, basis. So why not have instant access to the images we can capture without waiting for a film to develop? Let's take a look at the beginnings of camera technology.

The No. 1 Kodak Pocket camera was a cleverly designed unit which folded up into a relatively compact form. This example dates from around 1927.

It all began with the camera obscura

The camera obscura was simply a tiny hole in a sheet of material over a window in an otherwise darkened room. Rays of daylight would then project a reversed image of the scene outside the room on the opposite wall.

While the camera obscura was capable of creating a faithful image, there was no way of recording it other than manually with a pen or paintbrush.

Photographic societies were very popular in the early part of the 20th century, awarding plaques for prize-winning work.

Unfortunately, photosensitive chemicals, the active components in camera film, were not around until the 18th century. The seeds were sown, however, when a light-sensitive chemical was created accidentally in the 1720s from mixing chalk, nitric acid and silver in a flask.

Sunshine and silver

It was not until the early 1800s that such chemicals were used for recording images. One of the early pioneers was Thomas Wedgwood, who made pictures by placing objects onto sheets of leather that had been soaked in silver nitrate, and then left out in the sun to dry. Then in 1816 a camera obscura was constructed which used photosensitive paper.

The Kodak Box Brownie brought photography within reach of the masses.

Daguerreotype process and wet plates

During the 1830s these rudimentary processing techniques gradually improved with the use of contact printing and various light sensitive compounds, including silver chloride and silver iodide. One of these early methods was the 'Daguerreotype process', a method developed by the Frenchman Louis Daguerre. This process used highly toxic chemicals, including mercury, to create images on metal plates.

A much improved commercial process was developed in the 1850s in London called 'wet plate collodion photography'. It was much cheaper than previous methods, since it permitted unlimited reproductions to be made.

Cameras to the masses

Kodak was one of the first big camera companies, producing several pioneering models from the late 1880s onwards. The most famous of these was the Box Brownie – the first truly mass produced camera.

Colour, digital, what next?

In 1907 the first commercial colour film was produced, followed by the first multi-layered colour film in 1936 with the development of Kodachrome. In the early 1950s, the first video tape recorders converted live colour images from television cameras into digital impulses and saved them onto magnetic tape.

The first electronic camera was patented by Texas Instruments in 1972, although it was Sony which actually produced the first commercial electronic camera in the early 1980s. Apple were the first to manufacture a digital camera suitable for the home computer user, in February 1994.

The desire to make cameras smaller is not a recent phenomenon. This Halina Micro camera dates from the 1970s.

WHAT IS A DIGITAL PHOTO?

When a digital photograph is taken, an array of sensors capture the image and convert it into a series of electronic pulses that are stored in a digital form.

A photograph in a file

Electronic pulses are compiled into an electronic file for storage within the digital camera. There are many different formats for this storage, including JPEG, GIF, BMP and TIFF files, which will be examined in more detail later. The contents of the digital file can be opened with an imaging program such as Jasc's Paint Shop Pro or Adobe's Photoshop, of which

Once you download your images onto a computer, there are various programs available to enhance or manipulate them.

more later. These programs can also be used to manipulate the image, if required.

Once the image is in the required form – the right size, correct colouring and so on – it may be printed onto paper, imported into electronic documents, used on websites, as screensavers or for publication in magazines and newspapers.

Pixels and quality

The quality of a photograph itself is controlled by a number of factors, including the

Perhaps the easiest way to understand pixels is to look at a mosaic. Each tile corresponds to one pixel.

photographer, and, of course, the equipment used. Where digital cameras are concerned, this is largely dictated by the number of pixels contained within the picture. The word 'pixel' is short for 'picture element', and every digital picture is composed of thousands or even millions of pixels.

Actual vs effective pixels

Most digital cameras that are suitable for the amateur photographer are able to offer up to around 5 million pixels. It is important to understand the difference between the promoted 'actual number of pixels' and the stated 'effective number of pixels'. What you need to pay attention to is how many are actually used in making up your pictures – the effective number of pixels; this is what defines the quality of the camera.

DIGITAL VS FILM

Until recently, film cameras were better than the digital alternative, since film produced pictures of a far superior quality. However, this has changed with the introduction of higher resolution and reasonably priced digital cameras.

New resolutions

As the cost of digital cameras has plummeted, at the same time resolution has improved enormously. In the early digital cameras, 'resolution' was achieved in two ways: by direct imaging – taking the picture through the lens – and also by using software to

'improve' the quality of the photograph. Unfortunately, many claims were made for this technique, but most were exaggerated. Luckily for those of us

Improvements in digital camera technology have meant that even beginners can take high-quality shots – whatever the situation.

TIP: Deciding whether you like the shot enough to keep it is useful if you are short of camera storage space. If the results are poor you can delete the image and free up space on the memory card.

who use digital cameras, improvements in sensor technology have meant that we can now choose between many high-quality products that are on offer at affordable prices.

Instant gratification

Digital cameras also favour beginners – not only are they easy to use, but once you have taken a photograph you can look at your results almost instantaneously. With film cameras you would expect to have to wait for, at best, an hour to get your film developed before knowing whether you chose the best setting for your shot. With digital, you can view the shot straight away – and then retake it if you unwittingly got it wrong the first time…

Critical timing

All is not rosy in the world of digital cameras, however. One of the main criticisms is the time they need to acquire all the information to take a picture, which can often result in the shot being missed. One of the beauties of photography is that it allows a brief moment in time to be captured for posterity. Sadly, this moment can be all too brief, and the slower reaction time of the digital camera may mean that the shutter operates after the event has happened and the moment is missed. While this is often heralded as the great weakness of digital photography, there are ways around it, such as pre-focussing the camera as much as is practicable. If this is done correctly, the camera will respond just as quickly as any film camera.

Bursting the lag problem

There is another method of getting around the 'lag time' of digital cameras, and this is to use a rapid sequence mode. This is where the camera takes a short burst of pictures in quick succession. This can be useful for those occasions when things are happening too quickly to take individual shots, such as when the groom kisses the bride outside the church.

No more lost films!

There are many other advantages of becoming a digital camera devotee. For instance, how many of us know someone who has had a film processing company lose one of their films? In some

TIP: If you want to make sure you can capture sudden moments in time, then opt for a more expensive camera, which can give you about three frames per second.

Before the advent of the rapid sequence mode in digital cameras, capturing this image would be very hit and miss.

circumstances this can just be annoying, but if the film is of an important occasion like a wedding or funeral, then the loss can be heartbreaking. Likewise, the automated machines used by film processing companies can sometimes malfunction, which may result in the damage or destruction of a customer's film. This is, of course, not an issue with film-less digital cameras. Before the advent of digital cameras, you had no choice if you wanted to process your own films – you needed a darkroom. This is not only expensive, but it also means that you need to find a suitable place to set all the equipment up. These days, all you need is a computer and a few associated peripherals, such as a printer.

TYPES OF CAMERAS

Digital cameras can be divided into three main groups: those for professional use, cameras aimed at the keen amateur and those for the beginner.

Professional-use cameras

The cheaper professional-use cameras have similar resolutions to those aimed at the keen amateur at

around 5–6 million pixels, but with greater setting control and much better lenses. At the top end of the market, resolutions exceed 11 million pixels. Most current high-end models will accept film camera lenses.

The Canon EOS 10D is aimed at the well-heeled amateur or jobbing professional.

Amateur-use cameras

These models generally offer a blend of ease of use and reasonably high specification components. For the more experienced operator, they can have a lot of settings, but don't have the wide control range of the professional cameras. The better models have in excess of 5 million pixels, but have fully automatic functions for those who are still learning the ropes.

Compact carriers

One of the advantages that cameras in this category have over the professional range is that they are much smaller and lighter, making them more convenient to carry around.

Compact carriers offer reasonable quality at an affordable price. There is a huge market for this type of camera.

Budget cameras

Budget digital cameras are aimed at those users who are looking to start photography but do not want to spend a fortune before they know what they are doing, as well as the occasional 'snapper'. Choices can be made from among several disposable models, as well as those

The Coolpix range by Nikon offers a variety of inexpensive options.

incorporated into other devices such as mobile phones. These economy models are sometimes known as 'point and shoot cameras' and are mostly intended for taking impulse snaps on the spur of the moment.

WHAT YOU NEED TO GET STARTED

In this section we will look at what is needed to spend a day taking photographs. There are lots of accessories available, but most can wait until you know more about what you are doing.

Batteries Whichever model of digital camera you have, sooner or later your batteries are going to run flat. If the batteries for your camera are disposable, it is well worth investing in a set of re-chargeable ones.

Camera case A good case is vital to protect your camera from getting damaged. The more expensive types incorporate padding in case they are dropped.

Memory cards The general rule of thumb is that you can never have too much memory! Invest in large capacity memory cards when you buy your camera.

Connection leads The most important connection lead is the one that connects your camera to a computer for downloading pictures.

Download software If you purchased your camera new, it will have come with a CD containing all the necessary software for it to communicate with your computer. These programs are simple to use, since they more or less install themselves once the CD is in your computer. If you bought your camera second-hand and the CD is missing, you can normally download the software you need from the manufacturer's website.

Image manipulation There are many different kinds of image manipulating packages available, but if all you want to do is start off by taking some pictures, you will not need these programs yet.

Computer There are two main types of computer in use – PCs (which stands for 'personal computers') and Apple Macintoshes. Check whether the operating system – the software which runs the computer – is compatible with the programs that communicate with your camera.

Printer If you already own a computer for domestic or work purposes, the chances are that you will also already own a printer.

Scanner Although a scanner might seem an unlikely piece of kit to have, if you are using image manipulation software for your digitally taken pictures, you can scan in old, faded photographs and improve their quality using the manipulation software. You can then download them onto your camera for taking around with you and sharing with friends and family.

DIGITAL BASICS

Digital cameras are fun and generally easy to use. If you are already familiar with computers, then there really is not much to hold you back from mastering the basics very quickly.

IMAGE STORAGE & SAVING ISSUES

When you take a picture with a digital camera, it is stored in what is known as 'memory'. This is an arrangement of silicon chips that can record information in exactly the same way as computers.

Image storage for your camera

There are several types of digital camera memory, but for the purposes of generalization they can be divided into four basic

This is a typical digital camera memory card.

categories – fixed format, card format, disk format and tape format. The kind that you select or that comes with your camera will depend on the model.

Fixed format memory is sometimes also referred to as 'on-board memory' – basically, it means that the images are stored on the camera hardware.

Card format memory is what you will find on the vast majority of medium- to high-price cameras these days. Cards can be removed and replaced in seconds.

Take too many high-quality, large close-up pictures like this one, and you might run out of memory!

Disk format refers to mini CDs which are used by some camera manufacturers.

Downloading your photographs

When you have taken your pictures on your digital camera, sooner or later you are going to want to make use of them. However, before you can do this, you need to get them out of the camera. The usual method of saving your digital images is by connecting your camera to a computer and then transferring them across. This process is known as 'downloading'. Once you have completed the procedure, you will find that you have quite a choice as to what you do with your pictures!

Card types

The number of different memory cards on the market can seem quite bewildering to a novice photographer.

CompactFlash is the most popular card; these devices are, as the name would suggest, very small.

Flash cards are memory devices made using solid state computer chips. They have many plus points: they use very little power; they don't require batteries to store your images; and they are very small.

Microdrives are quite distinct from other memory devices in that instead of using computer chips, they have a rotating disc inside. This has the benefit of allowing very high storage capacities.

SD cards are very similar to CompactFlash cards, but they are physically smaller. There is another version of

the SD card available called the MultiMedia card. These are lighter, and are often used in

The MultiMedia card is a cheaper, lighter version of the SD card.

budget cameras and camera phones, which require particularly compact technology.

Mini drives

These wonderful devices are sometimes also known as 'data pens'. They are basically tiny units, only about the size of a key fob. They contain solid state memory, and have a USB plug on one

The USB data pen or mini drive is an excellent portable storage device.

end so that they can be plugged directly into a computer without needing to turn it off and back on again. They are a very convenient way of carrying large amounts of data around.

Storage for your computer

Hard disk drives are available these days with enormous storage capacities – over 200GB units are available. However, if they are your preferred storage method, you will need to ensure that you are not wasting disk space by using inefficient storage formats. Also, make sure that you have a back-up copy of your pictures somewhere; this is because computer hard drives can and do fail, and there is nothing worse than losing all your images as a result.

CDs and DVDs

If you prefer not to cram your computer's hard drive with digital images – or you are worried that it might fail – the most popular alternative storage medium to choose is the compact disc. A compact disc (CD for short) can store 650MB, which is enough for about 50 medium resolution images. CDs have the advantage of being cheap, reliable, easy to use and even easier to store.

If you have a CD or DVD writer, then you will need the right software to operate it.

The DVD (digital video disc) is a derivative of the standard CD with a much larger storage capacity. These discs can accommodate digital video as well as still images.

TIP: The recording surface of CDs should be treated very carefully – fingerprints, stains and scratches will degrade the disc, and data could be lost.

Methods of downloading

There are two basic methods of getting your digital images from your camera onto a computer. If your model has a memory card, you have the option of removing it from the camera and plugging it into a card reader – which is itself plugged into your computer. You can also use a download cable to connect the camera directly to the computer.

Before you download your images, you will need to ensure that your computer has the necessary software.

To install the camera's software, all you have to do is put the CD in the computer and the driver installation program will automatically start up. Then simply follow the instructions on the screen.

Once your computer has the necessary software installed, you need to find the right port for the download cable, whether USB or FireWire – usually at the back of the computer.

Some card readers make use of a high speed connection known as 'FireWire'. Here a reader is shown with a card fitted.

Folders and filenames

One of the things to watch out for when saving pictures onto your computer is that, unless you are very careful, it can be extremely easy to over-write existing files. This is because some cameras give you little or no control over the filenames of your pictures. For this reason, it is a good idea always to create a new folder when you are saving images. Another good idea is to add the date to the name you assign to the folder, as it is easy to forget naming conventions.

When you download images to your computer, it is a good idea to create a new folder with a suitable name each time. This will help you to keep track of your photographs in the future.

Canon

Canon Utilities
ZoomBrowser EX

Version 4.1 Copyright CANON INC. 1996-2003

When a lot of programs start up, they show an image
known as a 'splash screen'. This one is for Canon's
download package called 'ZoomBrowser'.

Image viewing

Once you have successfully saved your images to
your computer's hard drive, you will need a method
of viewing them. It is possible to use the computer's
file manager to display a list of the files; you can then
view each file by double-clicking on it, but this is a
particularly ponderous process. It is much easier to
use a special program to display your images as a
series of thumbnails. These software packages enable
you to click on individual thumbnails and then
enlarge them or manipulate them as you see fit. We
will examine this topic in detail later on.

Uploading images to your camera

Some of the better cameras available – that is, the mid-range models upwards – have the ability to load pictures from your computer onto your camera; this is known as 'uploading'.

Uploading can be a very useful feature. For example, if you are working away from home and have access to a computer, you can download all your images onto

If you want to upload images from your computer onto your camera, then you will need the necessary software. Canon's ZoomBrowser package is supplied with several of its models. This has a complete upload facility, as shown here.

the hard drive and view them at large sizes on a monitor. You could then spend several days shooting even more pictures of everything in sight, and by downloading them whenever your cards fill up, you could then reformat the cards each time. This is quicker than erasing the images, and is a good method of cleaning up old and overfull memory cards.

Once the images have been selected for uploading, ZoomBrowser offers you the option to resize them before transferral from your computer to your camera.

Following this procedure means you will never have to worry about running out of card space. It is inevitable, though, that many of your shots will not be good enough to keep. However, when you review them, you can be very selective about which ones you take home, and have the added advantage of being able to upload them to your camera. This method of carrying pictures is also ideal if you want to show a series of images to a group of friends: just connect your camera into a television set with a tv lead, and off you go!

IMAGES & PIXELS

All the digital images that you take are made up of minute individual components named pixels. In order to appreciate fully how your images work, you first need to understand pixels.

The significance of pixels

Since digital cameras take photographs that are composed entirely of individual pixels, it is worth taking the time to understand their significance. If you are going to take a series of images, it is sensible to set the camera's resolution to suit the purpose of the pictures, and this is where pixels come in. If you are only going to use the images for low resolution situations, such as website advertisements where the file size is likely to be less than 100KB, then there is no point in using a setting that will result in a 15MB file. If you are new to kilobytes (KB) and megabytes (MB), let me explain that there are one thousand kilobytes to every megabyte. That means that for every picture taken at a 15MB resolution, you could have 150 pictures at a 100KB resolution.

TIP: When buying a digital camera, choose one which offers at least one megapixel. If you can afford a model with more, so much the better – it will show in the quality of your images.

Image compression

When a camera processes a picture before storing it, the image is compressed. A good example of image compression is when a photograph is taken of something that has a lot of the same colour in it – for example, the walls of a room. The compression would then be able to reduce the information required to represent the image because it would not have to store a different colour for every part of the picture. However, too much compression results in image degradation.

Finally, high compression has been applied, and it can be seen clearly that the image is beginning to break up badly.

This Ferrari racing car is shown at three levels of compression – firstly with low compression...

...and then with moderate compression. Here it can be seen that the image is starting to degrade.

Image formats

If you examine a list of computer files, you will see that they are each composed of a name followed by a full stop and three letters. These three letters are known as the 'file extension', and they describe to the computer what sort of file it is dealing with. Digital images can be stored in several different ways – these are known as 'formats'. Each type is given a different name and the file extension is usually an abbreviation of this.

JPEG or JPG is the commonest format for image storage, and is usually the default output type of most cameras. If you want to send an image by e-mail, JPEG format is the one to use.

When you open up a folder you can view the contents as a series of icons or as a list of filenames.

The bitmap or bmp image format was originally developed for monochromatic images in the days before colour monitors and printers became widely available. Microsoft still uses this format widely.

Tag Image File Format or TIFF makes it possible to produce the very high quality images needed for publication purposes. Unfortunately, files saved in TIFF format tend to be large, so they can be inconvenient to handle.

Website designers prefer small-size, manageable image formats such as JPEGs or GIFs.

The Graphic Interchange Format or GIF can produce fairly high quality images for small file sizes. This has made GIFs popular with website designers.

RAW format images are created when a camera stores a photograph with no compression or processing being performed. This means that the image has to be handled by a suitable program if you want to view it on a computer.

BUYING EQUIPMENT

One of the advantages of digital photography is that you can zoom in on your downloaded pictures using your editing software. When you do this, sadly the image is not always as crystal clear as it looked on the LCD monitor when you took it. This might be the time to add some decent ancillary gear – perhaps a tripod or a flash gun – to improve your results.

IDENTIFYING YOUR NEEDS

While, of course, you want to buy the best equipment you can afford, there is no point in spending a fortune on sophisticated features you may never use. Identify your needs before buying.

Hard choices

Deciding just what you need in a camera may be a simple task for you, or it may be fraught with all manner of caveats, depending on your situation and the images you want.

Before setting your heart on a particular model, it is a good idea to go to a camera shop to see whether you can reach the controls!

Resolving your needs

If you are trying to decide which camera model to buy, then I would suggest you first consider what it is you really need it for.

Unusual circumstances require special photographic equipment.

Are you mainly going to be photographing your kids? Perhaps you are a keen botanist and would like to be able to capture shots of wildflowers in their natural environment? Either way, you will still need to decide what sort of quality you need. If your images are going to be used purely for websites, then you don't need a high specification camera, and you can save yourself a lot of money.

If you want to take lots of close-up photos of, say, wildflowers, then it makes sense to invest in a camera with a decent macro mode.

Even if it is only a basic point and click shapshot you are taking, the digital LCD on your camera means you can get it right nearly every time.

In general, a camera with 1–2 million pixels (1–2 megapixels) will be more than adequate. If your work is going to be published in magazine or book format, however, then things are very different, and you will need the highest resolution you can afford, with 4 million pixels (4 megapixels) being a sensible minimum.

Reviewing

Other features to check out are things such as whether you want an LCD viewing screen or not. While these are power hungry items, personally I cannot imagine

On compact digital cameras, you can use the LCD viewing screen for choosing your shot as well as for reviewing your images.

No matter what operating system you use, it is worth making sure that your computer has a good video card and monitor for really accurate colour reproduction.

being without one any more! LCDs tend to be between 4–6cm (1½–2½in) across, although for once size is not everything – the image quality can vary significantly. The most useful thing about having a screen is that you can review pictures as soon as you have taken them. This can save a lot of heartache!

Reaching the controls

Before you go rushing out and buying a particular model, it is vitally important to check that you can hold it properly. People with big hands need to consider whether they can access all the functions without pressing the wrong buttons all the time. Conversely, people with small hands need to ensure that they can reach the controls in the first place! Always make sure that the layout of the camera controls is to your liking before making your purchase.

If you have ever wondered why it is important to use a
suitable resolution setting on your camera, here is the
answer. Above are two photographs of a hand-coloured
illustration of moths. The main image above was taken at
2,592 x 1,944 on a 'Superfine' setting, whereas the image
on the opposite page was taken at 640 x 480 on a
'Normal' setting. From a distance, it is hard to distinguish
between the two, but when you zoom in [smaller images
above, top left and right], the differences are clear to see.

Features and modes

When you have worked out exactly what you want
to do with your camera once you have bought it, you
will need to check out the models that fit your
criteria. This can be a daunting task, as it can seem
that every one of them has a range of
incomprehensible features and modes. In order to
guide you through this maze of jargon, here is a quick

guide to the essential terms. Check the Glossary on pages 182–5 for further explanation.

Pixels and resolution Basically, the more pixels there are in your image, the better the resulting image will be. Two million pixels (2 megapixels) is about the minimum resolution you should settle for in the camera you select unless you only want to take low quality photographs.

Integral flash Unless you are only ever going to take pictures in well-lit areas, do not even think of buying a camera without a built-in flash or you will end up taking lots of very dark photographs!

Macro mode If the cameras you are looking at have a zoom facility, the odds are that they will all come with a macro mode. This allows you to take close-up pictures. Choose the best you can afford.

Red-eye reduction This is a mode in which the flash is fired twice in quick succession, causing the irises of the subject's eyes to close just before the picture is taken, eliminating most of the red eye reflections that are so common in flash photographs.

Zoom Beware! There are two types of zoom – optical and digital. Digital zoom is a method of magnifying

With a high quality optical zoom mode, you will be able to close in effectively on even the most distant objects. In the picture below, only the balloons in the centre of the original image are the subject of the zoom.

the image with clever processing techniques, but it falls short of the mark when compared to optical zoom, where all the magnification is performed by the camera lens itself. Ideally, go for optical zoom – with experience you will get visibly better results.

WHERE TO BUY GEAR

When the time comes to actually make a purchase, it is very important to ensure that you choose the right place to buy from.

Is it the best price? Something to watch out for is that while some cameras are advertised as bargain offers, the truth may be that the deal is not as good as

it seems. Often you will find that you have to buy much essential ancillary equipment separately.

Supplier location and aftersales service It is important to consider where you will be able to turn if your new camera goes wrong, as digital cameras, like other electrical products, do occasionally malfunction.

The internet is a superb tool, but you should always check carefully who you are dealing with.

The internet If you do not live near a city, or would prefer not to use a local outlet for whatever

Take geographical issues into account when buying a camera. If you live on an island, you are likely to be far more interested in mail order than someone who lives in a city.

reason, then there are many digital photography forums on the internet where you can get very good advice from true enthusiasts.

Credit cards If you have a credit card, it is a good idea to use it when you make your purchase, since you will automatically have a certain degree of insurance and other benefits.

Mail order If you read through the magazine adverts, you will soon get a feel for what deals are on offer for the cameras you are interested in – but watch out for steep postage costs and long delivery times.

Doing your homework It is worth doing your homework if you care about value for money. Check out the digital camera reviews in photography magazines.

TRIPODS & MONOPODS

If you are having trouble taking pin-sharp, crystal-clear images, it might be because your hands are shaking. A tripod or monopod will solve the problem. As the name would suggest, a tripod has three legs, although there are variants on the theme such as monopods, which have only one. If you have not used a support device before, it is worth borrowing one to see whether the improvement in picture quality really justifies the cost and inconvenience of buying one and using it regularly.

This super-light carbon fibre tripod is designed for maximum performance with the minimum weight.

Stability is all-important

The whole point of a tripod is to provide stability, but if you are going to be taking a lot of pictures on the move – of wildlife, for example – then you will also need one that is light and easy to carry yet very sturdy and resistant to knocks as well.

TIP: The platform for the camera at the top of a tripod is known as the 'head'. Take care when adjusting the head, as it is easy to wind it too far and see the camera crash to the floor.

CARD READERS

While it is possible to connect your camera to a computer to download your images, there are likely to be many occasions when this is just not convenient. Maybe the camera's batteries are flat, someone else is using it, or you simply don't have the camera with you – only its memory card.

In this case, what you need is a card reader. These are very useful little devices that generally plug into a computer's USB port either directly or via an extension cable.

Card readers normally connect to a computer through a USB port, as can be seen here.

Size matters

Considering the cost of many camera peripherals, as a rule card readers are good value for money. Most will fit in your pocket, which makes them very practical for travelling.

Card compatibility

Many types of card readers are available – some are dedicated to one type of card only, whereas others will accept between two and eight different formats.

CAMERA BATTERIES

Digital information cannot be stored or transferred without electrical power, so in the case of a portable digital camera its batteries are its lifeblood.

Flat batteries

One of the most frustrating things you can experience when using a digital camera is when you are miles from home and your camera's battery suddenly goes flat... There are various things you can do to try to prevent this problem from spoiling your day's photography. The simplest solution is to carry at least one spare battery with you, and to make sure that any you have are fully charged when you leave home.

Other ways of charging

There are other options, but which of these apply to you will depend on

There are lots of different battery chargers on the market, and most are relatively inexpensive. Re-chargeable batteries mean that you do not have to keep buying replacements.

the kind of batteries that your camera is able to accept. If you are going to be using your camera for protracted periods of time in a location without mains electricity, you can always use a car battery charger lead – this plugs into the cigarette lighter socket.

All the marvellous versatility of a digital camera disappears without access to electricity.

Always get the correct batteries

Many cameras will only accept batteries that were specially made for them by the original manufacturers, in which case you will just have to accept that this is the cost of owning that particular model of camera. Check with the manufacturer's instructions if in any doubt.

Nickel-metal hydride batteries

Where you have a choice, use NiMH (Nickel-Metal Hydride) batteries. These are designed for equipment like digital cameras which use current very quickly, and will hold about three times the charge of an equivalent NiCd (Nickel-Cadmium) battery.

CASES & BAGS

Digital photography is not an especially cheap hobby, so it makes sense to protect your investment in costly electrical equipment by protecting it properly in bespoke cases and bags.

Camera cases, bags and straps

If you go to buy yourself a nice, shiny new camera, make sure that you get a case or bag for it as well! Not only will the camera be a lot safer, but it will be much easier to carry around. There are some things in particular which you will need to protect the camera from, with salt water and fine sand being top of the list.

The best cases offer enough space to carry lots of ancillary equipment as well as the camera.

Bags and cases are available in all sorts of different sizes and styles, with some of the more expensive ones even being designed to be used underwater. Most of the camera manufacturers supply cases for their models, but they are inclined to be more expensive than similar products supplied by specialist companies.

LENSES & FLASH GUNS

The quality of the lens in your camera has a huge bearing on the quality of the images that you will be able to take. A flash gun can help improve that quality.

Lenses

The vast majority of digital cameras have no provision for anything but the lens they are supplied with from new. However, the maximum image quality a camera can achieve will be dictated to a great extent by the quality of its lens, so if you have any choice in the matter, go for the best one you can afford.

Flash guns

When a photograph is taken in perfect conditions, no extra light is needed. However, those taken at other times will need assistance from some kind of artificial lighting. Normally, this is provided by a flash of some kind, either internal or a 'gun'.

A flash gun can provide a lot more light when you are shooting in difficult conditions and will improve the quality of your images.

TAKING PICTURES

Unless your first digital camera is an economy model with no adjustable features, the range of control settings on offer can seem quite daunting. In this section we examine the controls that you are likely to come across on your digital camera, and discuss what they can do for you when you are composing and taking your images.

SETTING CONTROLS

If you have used traditional film cameras before, then you will be familiar with most of the setting controls available on digital equipment.

If you get the exposure correct [left], you will reproduce accurate colours, but get it wrong [above left] and a washed-out look with pale colours and poor definition will be the result.

If you want your subject to really stand out, it is vital to get the focus and depth of field right. In this image the butterfly is in sharp focus (as shown in the close-up), whereas the background is blurred.

However, if you are completely new to photography, and want to do more than just produce the most standard of images, then read on...

Creative control

If you want to produce something a little different, like to experiment and would love to explore your artistic abilities, then getting to grips with the settings controls on your digital camera will not only be vital, but also potentially a lot of fun! There is a great deal more to most digital cameras than the automatic mode that comes as standard.

But what do these various digital camera settings control? Here is a brief explanation of what each of them does.

Exposure With manual exposure you can control the amount of light that is allowed to reach the image sensor – this will determine how light or dark your photograph will be once it has been taken. The exposure of your image is controlled by a combination of the aperture size and the shutter speed of the camera.

Focus With manual focus, you can choose which object or area of your subject you would like to be in sharpest focus. Good focus takes a lot of practice to perfect, but will repay the effort involved with more rewarding photographs.

Aperture The aperture is a small hole behind the lens through which the picture is taken. The size of the hole is varied by manual or automatic adjustment to allow more or less light in, as needed. Its diameter is measured by what is known as an 'F-stop'.

Shutter speed The time that the shutter remains open for is the shutter speed. The longer the shutter is open, the more light is allowed in, so for low light conditions, it is left open for longer.

All four images above were taken with a shutter speed of 1/250, and the aperture set to F3.5. It can be seen that as the ISO value is increased, more light is acquired by the sensor, making the image increasingly over-exposed.

White balance You can use the white balance setting to control the light that you are using to illuminate your subject and improve the colours in your image. White balance is discussed in more detail later in this book, on page 68.

ISO speed This feature measures the camera's light sensitivity. Usually the feature is self-adjusting, so you do not need to worry about correcting what is a very delicate balance in your camera.

COMPOSING IMAGES

There are no hard and fast rules when it comes to composition. There are, however, several general principles which can help take you from being an outright novice to having enough experience to go your own way.

Composing pictures of animals is difficult because they seldom keep still! This photo was taken from a high angle to get the perspective I wanted.

Horses for courses

The very first thing to consider is why you are taking your picture. Is it to record an event, such as a wedding? If so, the odds are that you will be distributing copies to family members, in which case the recipients will expect to see photographs in the usual format. However, if your images are going to be used in some sort of publication, you may well need to compose your shots to fit in with a 'house style'. In this case, care must be taken to learn exactly what this entails before you begin taking photographs, as many publishers often have very different requirements.

When the final use of your images is not dictated by other people, you can clearly do whatever you want in

One way to draw the viewer into your image is to put in lots of interesting detail.

terms of their composition. This is where you can test your creativity, and in doing so, have a lot of fun. The

facility to take and delete photos at will makes digital cameras particularly suited to this approach – you can experiment to your heart's content without

This dramatic action photo was shot from ground level to emphasize the scale of the scene and maximize the movement in the image.

When taking an image of a tall, narrow object, it is best to try and ensure that the whole structure can be seen.

having to worry about throwing away lots of expensive film.

Grabbing attention

To make your images stand out from the crowd, you need to catch the viewer's attention. You can do this in many ways: by using dramatic colours; by choosing an eye-catching subject; or by framing the subject itself in an unusual or visually stimulating way.

Background issues

When you are working out your next shot, take a close look at the way the major elements are going to appear in the resulting image before going too far. Strong lines can make or ruin a photograph, depending on how they are used. If you are working outdoors on scenery views, vertical lines can extend from things such as trees, lamp posts or buildings, and horizontal lines can come from horizons, roads, bridges, and so on. If, however, you are working on close-up shots, you need to be a little more careful about objects that you might not otherwise notice until you are back at your computer.

Staying on the level

Sooner or later you might want to take some photographs of large expanses of water – rivers, lakes or the ocean. It is one of the unwritten rules of artistry that things that appear level in nature should be portrayed level in pictures and photographs. When you have a

When you take photos of things that the eye expects to be horizontal, it is best to ensure that the viewer sees them at the expected angle.

subject that you want to highlight without being to obvious about it, you can play all sorts of visual tricks. For instance, you can use other parts of the scene to lead the eye to your intended element. Roads, tracks, rivers and hedges have all been used to good effect many, many times, so if you can come up with new and exciting ways of doing this, your pictures will score lots of extra points from onlookers!

Using space

Once you have got your subject in place and decided on the other important features, it is important to check out the empty spaces in your image. Used incorrectly, they can ruin your picture, but used properly, blank areas can really enhance the message you are trying to convey. For example, if a racing car is entering a long straight, and you want the viewer to see that there is nothing up ahead, show lots of track.

If you want to convey a sense of movement through a landscape, it is a good idea to use space to emphasize the point. Here the enormous size of a motor racing circuit is powerfully portrayed by capturing a racing car in a position that gives a real sense of scale to the place.

Similarly, any other attempt to indicate motion over distance – perhaps images of canoeists, cyclists, aeroplanes, trains and automobiles – can all be improved in this way. If you have no reason to show a large empty area, then find some way of filling it – skies can have clouds and fields can be populated by livestock. No-one need know that these things were all added later using your image manipulation software (see pages 105–11)!

Cropping can make or break an image. There is too much foreground in the top image, and too much empty space to the left in the bottom image.

Finding an angle

Another way of exploring your creative side is to make your subject more interesting by presenting it from unusual angles. Rather than taking a portrait from straight ahead, for example, use a chair or step ladder to get above your subject, or crouch down below it. This will immediately make the picture more intrinsically interesting.

The effect of this image of a toadstool [top] is transformed when it is taken from a different viewpoint [bottom].

If you are going to take a photograph of a tall narrow subject, such as a skyscraper or a pine tree, or a low, wide vista like an open landscape, then it is a good idea to match the aspect ratio of the resulting image to the subject. This is the ratio of the width of a picture to its height. For example, when a picture has an aspect ratio of 1:1, it is square, but at 2:1 it is twice as wide as it is tall. In other words, it helps to make the shape of the picture fit the shape of the subject.

Visual checks

Once you have got your layout and angles sorted out, it is important to check how your subject shows up with respect to the background – if their colours are similar, it may well be that you cannot distinguish one from the other. If so, this photograph will be a wasted effort, unless you can rearrange your angle, the lighting or the depth of field, to make them stand apart.

Balancing acts

Having good visual balance in an image simply means that all the elements in it are well distributed so that it does not look lop-sided, or top- or bottom-heavy. While there are likely to be times when you will want to do this deliberately (such as adding empty space to convey motion), most of the time you will need to be taking balance into account.

Losing your balance

Imbalance can be caused by many things other than object distribution – for instance, a predominance of strong colours on one side of your image can make the other side look dull and empty. Likewise, deep shadows can throw an otherwise well-composed image off balance. If this is the case, you will either need to wait for the light to change naturally, or you will require in-fill from another source, such as a flash gun or electric lamps.

The composition of this shot would be fine if it were not for the deep shadowing.

FOCUS

Getting the focus right is one of the most basic, but most difficult, operations in photography. Not only do you need the right lens in place, but there are a whole host of other factors to keep in mind.

Staying in focus There are two kinds of focus – physical and virtual. Physical focus is achieved using adjustments in the lens position, whereas virtual focus is performed by software in the camera's processor

Fixed focus budget cameras Many budget cameras have no facility for focus adjustment – they do a reasonable job so long as the subject is not too close or too far away. Due to

In the image on the left the subject stands out crystal clear against a completely blurred background. In the righthand image, the auto focus picked up on the background foliage instead of the subject, ruining the photograph.

their low prices and acceptable performance, disposable film cameras have become very popular in recent years.

Auto focus Once you move up from the budget sector, just about every digital camera has the provision for auto focus. This is a facility where the camera senses how far away the subject is, and sets the focus accordingly. Some of the better cameras allow you to set the focus point, whereas cheaper models will only pick up on whatever is in the centre of the image.

In this image the Snapdragon flowerheads are in clear focus, but the stone wall behind has lost some of its edge, making the flowers stand out.

Manual focus If your camera has a manual focus facility, it allows you to disable the camera's auto focus and take full control of matters. For a start, you can decide for yourself exactly where the focus point is going to be. It is not until you have mastered the art of getting really crisp edges to your subjects that you can start to exploit the depth of field for full dramatic effect.

EXPOSURE

It is clearly vital to make sure that your photographs are not too dark or too light; this is determined by what is known as the image's 'exposure'. When an image receives too much light, it is said to be over-exposed. If an image has too much light in it and becomes over-exposed, this results in a loss of colour. The end result is normally a photograph that, depending on the extent of the over-exposure, may seem to be composed entirely of a series of light greys and whites. Conversely, too little light will produce a dark feel to the image; this is known as under-exposure.

Seeing the light

The actual amount of light that is allowed into the camera and onto the sensor is controlled by two things – the size of the aperture and the amount of time that the shutter is open. When the exposure is being controlled by the camera, all the shutter speed and aperture settings are determined automatically. The camera's processor calculates the correct settings by measuring the scene's light levels via a special light-metering sensor. Just how accurately the exposure is determined will depend on many things, but the most important factor is which part of the scene is measured. Most cameras try to account for the fact that the sky is very bright, and so they bias the readings towards the

The shutter speed and aperture size determine the amount of light that reaches the image sensor. The top-left image was taken with a 1 second

shutter speed, which resulted in a completely over-exposed image; the top-right image is still badly over-exposed with a 0.5 second shutter speed; at 1/10th of a second's exposure (bottom right) the image is almost correct.

bottom of the picture, but usually give priority to the middle of the scene, on the basis that this is the most likely position for your main subject.

If you are in doubt about how well the automatic exposure setting on your camera is functioning, many models offer an exposure bracketing facility, in which a series of pictures are taken, each with a slightly different exposure. You can then look through them and choose the best image, according to your preferred exposure.

LIGHT

One of the most challenging things to get right in digital photography is the light. Not only is it important to get this right for the overall scene, but also for the shadows and detail features in your images.

Light temperatures

Photographers often talk about light in terms of its temperature. Light that is biased towards the red end of the spectrum is said to be warmer, whereas that which is shifted towards the blue end is said to be cooler. For example, household electric lights are redder than daylight, which is said to be cooler due to its blue content.

When the sky is very cloudy as here, it can be difficult to get enough light to take good pictures.

This shot of an indoor water fountain display at Watermouth Castle in the UK was taken without a flash. The coloured lights give the image an unusual feel.

Exposures and light

When photographs are taken in low light conditions, it is necessary to use longer exposure times to capture the maximum amount of available light. Under these circumstances it is vital that the camera is held steady, or else severe blurring will occur. A tripod is the usual answer, but in the absence of one, you may be able to find a stable surface upon which you can rest the camera. If this is the case, it is a good idea to use the self-timer to trigger the actual shot.

Flash photography

All except the most basic of digital cameras have a built-in flash. Unfortunately, it is only when you get to the more expensive models that there is the facility to

These stainless steel ice-cream making machines were very reflective to photograph, resulting in a lot of flare from the flash. The result is a fairly unsatisfactory image!

directly control an external flash gun. However, some of the in-built units do have several modes. The default setting is the automatic mode, in which the camera adjusts itself to deal with the ambient light conditions. This can usually be turned on and off very easily to suit the occasion. It is important to remember that the flash needs to recharge between shots; depending on the circumstances, this can take more than ten seconds on a mid-range camera.

Recently, I was asked to get a shot of Watermouth Bay in
north Devon, England. However, when I got there, a large
mass of cloud was blocking out the sun [top]. Since the
photograph was needed the next day, I had to wait until
the sun came out to take the shot [bottom]. You can see
how long it took for a gap between the clouds to appear
by the position of the tide-line.

PROBLEMS WITH 'RED EYE'

Anyone who has ever taken a flash photograph of a friend or relative will be familiar with the dreaded problem of 'red eye'. Unfortunately, this common condition occurs just as much in digital photography as with film, but it can be avoided.

Red eye mode

When light strikes the eye, a certain amount of it gets reflected back towards the camera – and in doing so it gets filtered by the internal structures of the machine. In the case of eyes that are adapted for use in daylight, this reflected light shows up as red, whereas in animals whose eyes have adapted to being able to see at night, the reflections may be other colours – such as green in dogs, for example.

In this shot [left], the flash has resulted in 'red eyes', as can be clearly seen in the close-up of the boy's face [above].

The red eye mode available on many digital cameras gets around this problem by giving the eye an initial burst of light, before producing a second flash while it actually takes the picture. The first burst of light causes the iris to close partially, which blocks most of the red light from being 'seen' by the camera.

In this shot the red eye mode has worked; the owl's eyes have been rendered in their natural colour.

One thing to take into consideration is that this contraction of the eye can make the person being photographed look less attractive in the resultant image, so if this worries you, do not use the red eye flash mode; instead, remove the red colour in the eyes of the subject by using your image manipulation software on the finished photograph.

There is a further mode now commonly used to control how the flash on digital cameras operates to reduce red eye. This is the 'flash synch', and it has two settings, which are known as the '1st and 2nd curtains'. In the '1st curtain' mode, the flash is fired at the beginning of the shutter opening, whereas in the '2nd curtain' mode it is fired just before the shutter closes.

ADJUSTING WHITE BALANCE

The 'white balance' facility on digital cameras is designed to counter colour 'temperatures' and to standardize colours, through several different modes.

Auto In auto mode, the camera deals with any colour balance changes itself.

Daylight or sunny This mode is the best choice when photographing in sunny outdoor locations.

Incandescent or tungsten This mode is the best under incandescent lighting.

Fluorescent & fluorescent H These modes are for use under fluorescent lighting.

Cloudy The best choice when photographing in cloudy conditions.

Flash The best choice for flash photography.

Top: Automatic white balance; middle: 'Flash' mode; bottom: 'Tungsten' mode.

REVIEWING & DELETING IMAGES

Being able to review and delete pictures on the LCD screen of your camera is one of the greatest advantages of digital photography. Depending on how your camera is configured, you can either get a quick review lasting a few seconds each time you take a shot, or you can set it so that you can take as long as you like.

Choosing which images to keep

I review my images firstly to check that the subjects are all in frame. Then I look for any other objects that might have unintentionally ended up in the shot – either in front of, or behind, my main targets. If I am satisfied at this point, I then use the review zoom button to close in on the main parts of the image. Next, I examine the edges of my subject for sharpness. If all is still satisfactory, I then look at the shadows, and check to see if I can make out sufficient detail. The other things I check for depend on the situation; for example, if I am photographing a butterfly, I might have managed to get all the technical details right, but the butterfly might have closed its wings or shifted position as the shutter closed. In this case I will try to re-shoot the image, following the same procedure. The golden rule is: NEVER be too hasty with the delete button!

CAMERA MODES

Digital cameras offer several different modes to facilitate many different kinds of photography. As a rule, the more you are able to spend on your camera, the more modes you will enjoy.

Close-up or macro photography

Macro photography is the technical name given to what is more widely known as close-up photography. The subject matter for close-ups is irrelevant – the choice is entirely your own! Many people like to take pictures of natural items in the countryside, as illustrated here – wildflowers, butterflies, fungi, leaves, and many other living things all make excellent subjects.

The right camera

If you have a fixed focus camera, forget it – macro photography will be out of your reach until you obtain more suitable equipment. If you have a mid-range digital camera, you may well have a macro mode, in which case you can make a start in this fascinating field of photography. If you are lucky enough to have a high-end camera, while you may not already own a specialist macro lens, there will certainly be several available to suit your model.

Unless you have one of these, you will soon find that there are real limitations to what you can and cannot achieve. Macro mode on a mid-range digital camera will allow you to capture images from distances of around 10cm (4in) up to about 50cm (20in).

Macro and compacts

A careful balance needs to be struck with cheaper compacts and cameras with limited macro modes. Take the picture from just too far away [top] and the image will begin to pixellate (break up into dots) when you use your imaging software to zoom in on it [inset].

Personally, I find that when I use a compact camera, I get the best results when I use the highest resolution setting at distances of around 50cm (20in) than I do when I try to shoot closer up. One of the best things about macro photography is that you can experiment endlessly –

Some compact cameras struggle to acquire a good focus
if you get too close to your target. To increase the number
of useable shots I get, I use a high resolution and stay a
bit further back when I frame the shot [top]. Once I have
got the picture I want, I use my imaging software to zoom
in on the subject [bottom].

the more things you try, the more you will learn, and this on its own may make the exercise worthwhile for you.

Portrait mode

Portrait mode sets the camera up to take images where the subject is in focus, and the background is blurred. We will examine this subject in detail later.

Self-timer mode

This picture of my little girl was taken with a disposable film camera without a self-timer mode. Pity – it would have been nice to be in it with her!

The self-timer allows you to take the picture and be in it at the same time. Most digital cameras have this facility. When set to this mode, you simply line the camera up, press the shutter release button, and get into position. The camera will usually beep quietly until it takes the shot.

TIP: There are other uses for the self-timer mode. For example, a timed release can allow you to improve the sharpness of your images. If you place the camera on a solid object and get it to self-release, you will avoid any camera shake, which is handy for sports or action photographs.

Auto mode

In the 'Auto' mode, as you would expect, most of the settings are controlled automatically by the digital camera, so if all you want to do is point the camera and take pictures, this is the mode for you. There are, however, several things that you can still do to enhance your images in this mode.

Firstly, you usually have the option to zoom in to the subject. Just how much you choose to zoom will depend on how close you are to the subject and how much of the background you think you should include. If you like the background, leave it in, on a high resolution – if not, you can

The subject of this image is off-centre [below left]. However, the problem is easily fixed with a software cropping tool [centre and top right].

crop it away later in your image manipulation software until you are happy with the results.

Manual mode

Once you have learnt the basics of how your digital camera works, you may well want to experiment with the photographic special effects that it offers. This is where setting the camera to manual comes in; essentially, this mode hands you control of both the shutter speed and the aperture size.

An ultra-slow shutter speed makes the most of a photograph of a waterfall.

Shutter speed priority mode

When the camera is set to shutter speed priority mode, the aperture size is still automatically controlled for the best exposure, but you get full control over the shutter speed. You may choose to do this so that you can set it to a very high speed for capturing moving objects, or alternatively you may want to go for a very slow shutter speed for subjects such as waterfalls.

Aperture priority mode

When you set the camera to aperture priority mode, it still calculates the best shutter speed to give you the optimal image exposure, but also allows you to adjust the aperture size to suit a particular effect. This can be very useful if you want to play around with depths of field – that is, the relative crispness of objects in the foreground and background of your image.

Stitch mode

You may well have seen images produced by panoramic film cameras before – such as school photographs, in which several hundred pupils line up in wide, massed ranks so that they can all be photographed together. How many of you remember the weird and wonderful cameras that slowly spun around on rotary mounts as they recorded your unhappy visages? Well, these days most of the better digital cameras can take similar pictures by using what is known as 'stitch' mode. This is where a series of overlapping images are re-processed by the camera into one extra-wide panoramic view.

Landscape mode

Landscape mode sets the camera up to shoot expansive scenes. It generally does not have quite the same range and flexibility as stitch mode, but it is an ideal medium for taking photographs of countryside scenes and so on.

This is a good example of a panoramic image taken in stitch mode, in which three overlapping sections of the overall image have been 'stitched' together digitally.

Low light mode

Low light or night scene mode allows you to capture an image where a close-up subject gets lit by the flash, but the rest of the scene is given a low shutter speed. This lightens the background to make it appear to match the foreground subject.

Auto-rotate mode

If your camera has an auto-rotate mode, it means that an orientation sensor is used to detect which way up the camera was held when a shot was taken. If the

Do not despair if your image turns out like the top one above – misty, dark, indistinct and generally very disappointing. The version beneath it has been adjusted using the sharpen, automatic saturation enhancement, brightness and contrast tools in an image manipulation software program on a computer. It is not perfect by any means, but it is much improved.

mode is in operation, it turns all the images through the appropriate number of degrees so that they are all the same way up when you review them. If you are displaying your images on a television set or computer monitor, this facility can be very useful indeed.

Photo effects mode

If your camera offers this mode you can shoot images with all sorts of interesting and exciting effects.

Vivid This effect enhances the colours and overall contrast to make the image seem brighter and sharper overall.

Neutral This feature does exactly the opposite of the 'Vivid' setting – it tones down the colours and contrast in the image.

Low sharpening This feature reduces the strength of the outlines of the subjects in the image to give them a softer look.

Sepia As you would imagine, sepia mode records the scene in sepia tones instead of full colour, enabling atmospheric image effects.

Black and white When this effect is applied, images are recorded in monochrome. Many people think that this is the best way to convey artistic images, feeling that the effects achieved are more subtle than colour.

Custom effects With the custom setting, you get full control over colour, contrast and image sharpness.

Fast action mode

The fast action mode is used for taking photographs of fast moving subjects such as cars and trains.

Slow action mode

The slow action mode is generally used for creating artistic shots with blurred images of moving objects.

It is ideal for photographing running water, especially waterfalls or waves.

Monochrome mode makes this image striking and moody. With a sepia effect applied, it becomes almost haunting and spooky, as the lighting in the image is subtly altered by the effect.

When you are photographing fast moving objects, use the fast action mode to increase the shutter speed of the camera and thus reduce blurring in the finished image.

Continuous shooting modes

Many digital cameras have their own version of the film camera's motor drive. There are two commonly available versions – low and high speed. Typically, the low speed continuous mode will allow you to see each image on the LCD screen as it is captured, whereas the high speed version does not. These modes are excellent if you want to take a series of shots of some kind of action event – a bowler at a cricket match, an overtaking manoeuvre in a car, a motorcycle or horse race, or simply your kids playing with the family pet! Only video mode (see Chapter 8, 'Digital Video') has greater flexibility.

EDITING IMAGES

In this chapter we look at storing and keeping track of your images, applying effects, and the formats that you may need to share your work with others.

ORGANIZING & ARCHIVING YOUR IMAGES

The storage methods used on digital cameras are another feature that make them more attractive than film cameras. Since the cards are very small and light, you can easily carry several spares, with enough capacity to hold thousands of images.

Holidays and full cards

When I am away on holiday, I always take more than one memory card with me. I can then go to a camera shop and pay for the images to be downloaded onto a CD whenever the cards start to fill up. Some shops will also provide you with an index sheet as part of the download operation. These have all your shots shown as 'thumbnails' – a mini image of each photo, which is very useful for cross-referencing (see opposite).

Most people have access to a computer, unless they are away from home, and will generally want to

If you ask a camera shop to download your images, you may receive a printed mini index gallery, as you do for film processing. This is very useful for cross-referencing.

download images themselves. This is a straightforward operation between most cameras and computers (see pages 24–5). The images stored on the memory card are shown as a mini gallery.

Downloading your images

Download programs will usually offer the facility to select any or all of the images for transferral, as well as the ability to delete any or all of them as desired. This is where a little organization is helpful....

Keeping track of images

If you have been using your camera for a while, you will find that it is hard to remember which folder holds which images. Create a series of folders with descriptive names and a date to help you.

IMAGE MANIPULATION

Good image manipulation software makes all the difference when working with digital photographs. Among the two most popular are Adobe Photoshop and Jasc Paint Shop Pro. Photoshop is the more powerful program, although a reduced version (Photoshop Elements or LE) is perfect for the beginner. Paint Shop Pro is less powerful than the full Photoshop version, but more affordable for the keen amateur.

Downsizing images

If you use a high resolution, when you download your images they will be very large. So the first thing to do is shrink them to suit your purposes – this is called 'resizing'. It is a good idea to leave the original image untouched, however, and to save a copy. This way, if you mess up the image, you still have the original from which you can make a further copy.

TIP: High resolution pictures can soon fill up a 32MB memory card. As well as taking a spare card, consider purchasing one with more capacity – anything up to 4GB!

Cropping

Once the image is a manageable size, the next job is to cut any unwanted edges away from the main subject – this is called 'Cropping'. Select the cropping tool from the tool palette. If it isn't visible, go to 'View', select 'Toolbars' and tick the 'Tool Palette' box. The palette will then appear down the left side of the screen. With the cropping tool selected, the mouse cursor will change from an arrow to what looks like two overlapping arrows. Position the cropping tool somewhere on the top left of the image (it doesn't matter where),

While the bike [top] looks good, there are bits of litter in the background, so it is time to crop the image down… The image has been opened in Paint Shop Pro, and the crop tool (the red frame) used to set the desired area [centre]. After double-clicking on the image, the program cut away the marked area, leaving the cropped image [bottom]. Litter and blue paint were also removed from the original image.

To shrink high resolution images to a manageable size – in Paint Shop Pro, for instance – open up the image, click 'Image', then 'Resize'. A dialog box allows you to set the parameters that control the image size. Save the image under another name, or you will lose the original, to which you might need to return. Here, a friendly seagull has been resized.

The beauty of cropping is that it allows you to create several different images out of one original or to improve a photograph that might have been taken in a hurry....

and hold the left mouse button down. Keeping it down, drag the tool across to somewhere on the bottom right, and then release the button. You will now have a thin black rectangle over your image. Using the mouse, position the four sides of the rectangle to correspond with the points where you would like the outside edges to be. When you are happy with the cropping lines, double-click the mouse anywhere on the image. The areas outside the crop lines will be removed and you will be left with a cropped image. If you are not happy with the results, go to 'Edit' and click on 'Undo Crop'. Alternatively, hold down the control key and press the 'z' key.

Compressing the image (Paint Shop Pro)

If you need to make the file sizes of your images small enough to send by e-mail, or to post on a website, then resizing and cropping your images will indeed make them smaller. However, there is another way to minimize the file size. This is known as compressing.

To compress an image file, open the image in Paint Shop Pro, select 'Edit' and then 'Save As'. A dialog box appears and you will see a button in the bottom right-hand corner of the box labelled 'Options'. If you click this, a second dialog box opens called 'Save Options'. You will see that there is

If your photos were taken at a high resolution and are still at full size, they will be far too big to e-mail. To reduce the file size, use file compression.

something called a 'slide bar' running from left to right across the box. At the left it says 'Lowest compression, best quality', and at the right it says 'Highest compression, lowest quality'. You will also see that there is an indicator arrow shaped like the end of a house. This can be dragged along the line using the

To use file compression, open the file up in your graphics program, and find the 'Save As' option. Select 'Options'. In this image we can see the options offered for a JPEG file.

mouse. It is worth experimenting to see exactly what effect this has on your image. Don't forget, however: never experiment with the original file. Always make a spare copy called 'My_Test_Image', for example, just in case it all goes horribly wrong!

The two extremes of the compression scale are easy to define. If you use maximum compression, you will get a very small file, but the quality will be so bad that you may have trouble recognizing it as your image. On the other hand, if you use maximum quality, the image size will hardly change. It is worth spending some time finding out which level of compression will best suit your task.

Zooming in

One of the most useful facilities that you will find in all the commercially available graphics packages is the ability to 'home in' on specific parts of your images. This is useful if you have taken a photograph quickly, without giving the final composition of your shot much thought. By zooming in, you can decide whether the focal point of the image is good enough to crop. While it is good to be able to check how sharp the focus is, the really useful aspect is that when you are re-touching an image, you can expand the image until you are looking at individual pixels. In other words, if you have got the time and patience, you can completely rebuild your image from scratch.

Zooming in allows a tighter focus on part of the main image.

Zooming out

The 'zoom out' facility can be very handy if you have an image that needs to be shrunk down for some purpose, such as posting it onto a website. It means that you can look at it on screen at the actual size it is going to end up at before you make any changes. By doing this, you can get an idea as to whether you need to perform any cropping, and whether you can get away with applying any compression without losing too much detail.

Rotate

Some digital cameras will automatically rotate your images so that whichever way up you hold the camera the shot always appears the right way up.

The rotate tool is great for re-aligning images that have been taken with the camera held at unusual angles for special effects.

Saving images in specific formats

If you are sending your images off to other people for use in websites, glossy magazines, enthusiast publications, or by family and friends, sooner or later you are going to be asked to use an image format that you are not familiar with. It may be that your

camera saves images in the JPEG format, for instance, and a magazine has asked you to supply images in the TIFF format, since this is what the publishing industry usually works with. If this is the case, find the original file (the unadulterated image) and make a further copy of it. You need

In order to retain the full quality of your original image, you need to be careful about which format you save it in.

to do this because if you have resized or compressed the image you will have lost a lot of the detail, and magazines need the highest possible quality for reproduction. Open this copied original, go to 'Edit', and click 'Save As'. Explore the list of formats offered, select the appropriate one, and then click 'Save' – and that is all there is to format conversion!

Blank out a number plate

You want to publish some photographs of a motorcycle on a website, but for security reasons, you do not want the number plate to appear. Firstly, resize and crop the image. In your graphics package, make sure you have the tool, colour and control palettes visible. Select the paintbrush tool and use the controls palette to choose the shape and size of the paintbrush. Next, choose the colour to 'paint' out the figures. Position the mouse pointer over the colour palette; as you move it around, the current colour is shown in a small box below the palette. When you have found the colour you want, click on it, and your chosen colour is displayed. Now you start painting by clicking on the image and dragging the paintbrush around.

The motorcycle with its number plate partly blanked out [left]. The same image with the numbers completely blanked out [centre]. The window which shows the various palettes needed to paint out the number plate [right].

Blowing in the wind...

There are a lot more things that can be done with a
graphics package than painting out letters. For
instance, I recently took this night shot in Portugal
of some ornamental grasses blowing in the wind. I
used a long exposure to give them a blurred effect.
If you have an artistic flair, or think you may have, it
is well worth taking an image and experimenting
with all the effects your particular graphics program

As it stands, this picture does not exactly grab your
attention, but look what happens over the following
three pages when you add some special effects.

Above, the same shot is modified with a chrome effect. This effect converts the image to what is known as a greyscale format. Effectively it is black and white, but it also does all sorts of other strange things. Notice how the spotlight goes from being a bright object to one that is completely black. The grasses themselves have been highlighted, and their stalks show up well.

can produce. The more recent releases have a stunning array of options that can make a huge difference to an image, but when they are combined, the sky is the limit! For a start, have you thought about what an image that is shot at night might look like when seen as a negative?

This is the same scene converted to a negative image. You could also convert an image to a negative form, and then include certain parts of it in a 'normal' photo.

The fade correction in this version has changed the colours dramatically – it has really brought out the greens in the grasses, but also added a blue haze around the flowerheads.

This version of the image has had the 'contour effect' applied to it. If you want to try something really surreal, it may be the ideal tool for the job!

An alternative to just applying a negative effect to the image is to apply another style on top of it. This version is a negative with a coloured foil effect applied.

Drawing attention

Sometimes when you look at your finished work, you may decide that the subject – or focal point – of the image is unclear and that you would like to give this feature more emphasis. Rather than simply cropping in to a feature in your photograph, which then effectively removes the rest of the image, you may wish to retain the entire scene but highlight the main focal point of interest.

In Paint Shop Pro, an effect that can draw attention to a particular element in your image is adding a magnifying lens. As with most of the other manipulation tricks that can be applied to an image in this software package, this effect can be adjusted to the smallest degree. This means that you are in control as to how big the magnifying lens appears and what degree of magnification is applied to the important element.

Adding a lens to the woman's face [inset] leaves you in no doubt as to the main focus of the image.

Getting framed

Once you have resized, cropped and compressed your image, you might want to give it a fancy frame. Here (above left) we have a picture of someone cleaning their mask mid-way through a paintballing session. In order to give the image a documentary feel, I have added a film slide effect, using the 'Picture Frame' command in Paint Shop Pro. We also have to face up to the fact that the flash has caused the famous 'red eye' effect, which has been removed using a graphics package.

Frame effects can change the mood of your images. In the bottom image I have also used the 'Red eye removal tool'.

Most graphics packages come with a variety of picture framing functions, including the film slide frame. Other framing styles include various picture frame effects – both modern and traditional, soft-focus frames – in many shapes, as well as a 'ripped-paper' effect to look as if the image has been torn from the page.

Getting rid of red eye

Lots of digital cameras on the market come with a red eye removal feature (see page 70). However, if your camera does not, then you can easily remove this

A close-up shows the red eye problem.

common problem by using image editing software. Most of these programs use a dedicated red eye removal feature. (Paint Shop Pro is featured here.) You can perform the function manually as well by zooming in on the individual pixels and recolouring them.

The red eye tool in Paint Shop Pro has several modes that allow you to zoom in and remove the red elements from the eye. Here, I have used the freehand outline facility to specify the area for attention. In the left window pane I have drawn around the reds, and the right window pane shows the results.

Distorting the truth

There are numerous effects that can be achieved using the inbuilt features of most image manipulation software. You can also buy or internet-download free hundreds of additional features.

Here, we have an example of image distortion. In this instance I have used an add-in (plug-in) for Paint Shop Pro called 'Gloop'. As you can see, you can make all sorts of alterations to any part of the image. I didn't have the heart to do this to any of my friends, so I picked on a harmless little reindeer instead...

With some rather unsubtle distortion, a cuddly soft toy [left] becomes a curiously mutated, monster reindeer!

Set in stone?

Photoshop comes with its own equivalent to Paint Shop Pro's 'Gloop' effect. With the 'Liquify' filter, you can distort any part of an image, making the image

look as if it has turned to liquid. In Photoshop Elements, go to the 'Filter' menu, find 'Liquify' in the pull-down menu and apply the liquify filter to whatever area you select on an image. With the cursor pressed down where you want the distortion to start, simply drag the particular feature to where you think is suitable within the image. As you can see from the images on these pages, the Liquify feature is great fun to play around with.

A swimmer performing the butterfly stroke looks impressive [top], but what could make him go even faster, just for fun? An added pair of flippers [bottom] should do the trick nicely!

Stretch it out

Another distortion filter that comes with most image manipulation software is the 'Pinch' effect. As its name suggests, it is almost as if a point of an image stretches or squeezes the entire image from the point of selection. In Photoshop Elements, when you choose 'Pinch' – which is found in the Filter menu under 'Distort' – a sliding scale bar will appear, as well as the part of the image to be distorted. The image snapshot allows you to gauge in real time what the overall effect will be when certain levels of pinch are applied.

An ordinary family group picture can be given a fun 'hall of mirrors' effect by applying the Pinch filter with a positive value. This is a great trick for jokey e-mails, or maybe birthday and Christmas cards.

The scale values in Pinch range from -100 to +100. Positive values squeeze the distortion towards the centre of the image; negative values shift or extrude it outwards. Practice makes perfect with this feature!

Artistic flair

Nowadays, image editing software is so sophisticated that it can take our photographs back to a time before cameras were invented and turn them into veritable works of art. Various artistic filters are available, producing effects that the finest Impressionist master would be proud of! The features produced include: a charcoal drawing effect; a crayon or pencil drawing effect; a filter that turns a picture into an oil painting or a watercolour; a sponge or smudge stick effect; and a rough pastel filter, which is the effect shown below. When you select any of these filters, you are given the option of how much of the effect you wish to apply to your image. The choice, of course, is entirely yours and will depend on the type of stylized effect that you wish to achieve.

A pleasant enough holiday shot that will look good in a family album [left] ... or a stylish pastel effect portrait to hang in a decent picture frame [right]?

Colour me... anything you like

Another effective manipulation technique is to replace the actual colours of an image with vastly different shades to create a completely different feel to an image, as we can see here in this picture of giraffes on the savannah at sunset. In Photoshop Elements, by choosing 'Replace Color', a dialog box appears. Click on the colour you want to replace in the preview window, then in the Transform section of the box, move the Hue slider

An atmospheric safari shot of giraffes silhouetted in the dying light of sunset...

...or perhaps you would prefer them at midnight? Simply replace the colour and you have an identical night shot.

scale to change the colour – in this case from orange to blue. Experiment with the Saturation and Lightness sliders until you have achieved the desired effect.

Detail, detail, detail

Inevitably, when you have downloaded your images onto the computer and have opened them up to view them, you may be a little disappointed by the lack of sharpness of some. The

detail of certain parts of the image may not have come out as clearly as you would have liked. Have no fear – image

The original image [above] did not have much definition to the brickwork or ornamentation around the doorway, which the sharpened image now shows clearly [left].

editing software is here! The Sharpen menu will pull pixels together, improving the definition of a fuzzy or hazy looking image. Sharpen More or Sharpen Edges may improve the image. However, it may make it look pixelated and even lose its resolution. Again, experiment with an image. You can always press Apple Z or Control Z to undo any changes to the image.

Saturation point

Another problem that you may have with your digital images is that they sometimes appear slightly washed out. This generally means that the colour is not as vibrant as you remember when you took the photograph in the first place. In Photoshop Elements, pull down the Enhance menu, go to Colour and select Hue/Saturation. In the dialog box, slide the Saturation scale to the right to increase the intensity of the colours. This will affect all colours in the image. If you wanted to concentrate on skin tones, for example, in the Edit menu at the top of the dialog box, select Reds and again slide the Saturation scale slightly to the left to adjust the tones.

Colour saturation in the editing software [bottom] transforms this dull, flat photograph [top].

PRINTING IMAGES

You are likely to want to print your photographs at some stage. In this chapter, we look at printers, ink cartridges and the other accessories you will need.

PRINTERS

Most of us who take digital photographs will want to print them on to paper for display in albums or picture frames at some stage, in order to make the

most of our images. Unless you are prepared to pay for someone else to provide image printing as a service – for example, a specialized photographic shop – sooner or later you are going to need to buy a printer and learn a little about the subject of printing. Broadly

This economical bubble jet printer can print around six sheets of text per minute, as well as reasonably good quality colour prints.

speaking, getting good prints of images is reliant on two things – the quality of the printer and the quality of the paper.

The CP-300 Canon Card Photo Printer is a truly portable device in that it can be run from battery power.

Printer types

Printers come in many forms: dot matrix, inkjet, bubble jet and laser are the most common types. Dot matrix printers are really only suitable for simple text output – things like shop receipts are often produced in this manner. Laser printers produce the highest quality prints, but while the black and white versions are practical for home use, colour versions can be very expensive. The most suitable choice for producing high quality photographic prints in the home is the inkjet printer, which uses a cartridge to drop ink directly onto the paper. Bubble jet printers, which are often cheaper, use special heating elements to prepare the ink. Portable printers that link straight to the camera are also available; these are known as photo printers.

TIP: Generally, inkjet printers are cheaper than lasers. However, a drawback is that they are considerably slower, which may be a problem if you are printing lots of photos.

Printer cartridges

No matter which type of printer you decide to use, to produce your image onto a sheet of photographic paper as a print it will need ink – and ink comes in the form of cartridges.

Colour cartridges are often made up of three colours, which are blended together to produce the different shades that make up a colour photo print.

Inkjets

Inkjet printers use two cartridges to supply the ink – one for black and the other for colour. Of the two, the black is cheaper to purchase than the colour cartridge. Most printers come with software that allows you to monitor the levels of ink. This can prove to be very useful, because you get advanced warning that you need to get spare cartridges before they actually run out.

Cartridge replacement

When a cartridge runs out, replacement is extremely straightforward on most printers. New cartridges are available from the original manufacturer, but can be rather expensive. Cheaper alternatives are often

Go for good quality ink cartridges for great results [left], as poor quality ink will often disappoint [below].

supplied by discount companies that specialize in undercutting the manufacturers. However, the old adage that 'you only get what you pay for' is worth remembering. Certain generic brands do not last as long and are not of the same high quality ink as those of the manufacturer's own-brand ink cartridges. This is fine for colour printing onto normal copier paper, but very noticeable when printing images onto high quality photo paper. The colour can vary and will cancel out all your hard work of retouching or enhancing the colour resolution of your images. Some people keep their empty ink cartridges for re-filling, either by a professional outfit or with a 'do it yourself' home refill kit.

Putting print to paper

Paper comes in many forms, but the two main variables are its finish and weight. The quality of paper suitable for printers is mainly dictated by the type of coating used – and its thickness.

Always check the labels of products carefully to make sure that the paper you are buying is the correct type for your needs.

Types of paper

The paper used for domestic purposes, such as printing out letters, is typically 80gsm, with 100gsm being a thicker, but more expensive alternative. High quality paper is available for photographic purposes and generally comes in small packs of between 25 and 100 sheets, as opposed to packs of 500 sheets in the case of general purpose paper. Photographic paper generally has a glossy coating on one side. Load the paper into the printer so that this is the side which the print ends up on, as otherwise the quality of the print will be considerably degraded!

If you have a photo quality printer, you will need to ensure that you use the right kind of paper, such as this photo paper [above], when printing your photographs out or else you may get extremely poor results.

If you normally use general purpose paper, whenever you want to use special purpose media such as photo quality film, you must reset the printer properties to let it know that you are using something different; otherwise, your prints will look very mediocre.

Choice selection

Look out for 'sustainable forest' labels, some of which state that the paper is 'made entirely from pulp obtained from 100% farmed trees' or similar. This means you are buying an ecologically sound product. If paper is recycled, this will normally also be highlighted on the paper's packaging. Look for the standard green recycling logo.

Special quality paper should be stored away from sunlight and extremes of temperature, and any prints you make should be kept in resealable bags to protect them from humidity, sunlight and temperature variations.

If you want to be environmentally friendly, look for recycling logos, which indicate that the paper you are buying has been produced from reusable sources.

It can be confusing looking through all the different types of paper on the market, so here are a few of the types you may come across:

Photo quality glossy film A bright, white film; good for photos, and report covers. Generally available in A2, A3, A4, Letter and Super A3/B sizes.

Inkjet transparencies Available in A4 and Letter; clear films producing excellent colours for overhead projections and overlays for presentations.

Inkjet cards Bright, white A6 cards; excellent for creating postcards, snapshots, invitations, and digital photos, for example.

Connecting to a printer

For converting your digital image into something tangible that you can show friends, you need to get your image over to a printer.

Transferring images to a printer

There are basically two methods of getting images from a digital camera onto a printer. The simplest method is to use a direct cable connection between camera and printer. While this is very straightforward, the disadvantage is that only certain printers have the special socket which allows the direct connection to be made. The most obvious devices are the portable photo printers mentioned on page 113. The other (and by far the most widely used) method for printing an image is to download it onto a computer, and then use whatever printer is linked to the computer. This is a much more flexible approach. You can then make prints of your images at any time.

Photo printers produce prints direct from the camera via a connection lead linking the two devices.

Printer software

When you buy a new printer, you have to make sure it can communicate with your computer. Some operating systems will be able to do so without any further software, but usually you will need to install the manufacturer's own drivers.

Printer drivers

When a new printer is installed, it must be able to find the correct software on the computer in order for it to

When you print an image out in Paint Shop Pro, this is the dialog box you will see as you click the 'Print' icon. It allows you to specify the number of copies you want, as well as the size, orientation and position of the image.

work properly; this is known as the 'driver' and controls how documents from your computer print out. The drivers for many printers come as a standard feature on some operating systems, whereas others need to be specially installed. New printers will come with the drivers supplied on CD. These are easy to install, since the disk will auto-start when it is inserted into a computer. The set up procedure is simply a matter of following the instructions on the screen. If the disk is

The printer driver will ensure that the correct messages are sent from the computer to the printer, in the form of electrically conveyed digital information.

missing – maybe the printer is second-hand or the original has been lost – a search on the internet will usually prove fruitful. Personally, I use Google (www.google.com) as my search engine. If you enter the name of the printer together with the words 'free download' and 'driver' in the Search field, it will nearly always result in what you need in order to get your printer 'talking' to your computer.

COMPUTER OVERVIEW

So many of us use computers these days that they have become a feature of just about every household and office. Nevertheless, it is worth considering which models are likely to be the most suitable for your needs.

Hardware issues

Compaq produce several desktop computers, such as the Presario 8000.

If you already have a home computer, it will probably be entirely adequate for your purposes. Processor speeds are usually above 2GHz, but you will not need one this fast unless you do a lot of image processing.

Memory sizes

Far more important than processor speed is the amount of RAM you have. This is the solid state memory the computer uses when doing any processor intensive operations. Start with a minimum

---

TIP: The 'processor' is what determines the speed of your computer – the larger the number, the faster it will go. 'RAM' is 'Random Access Memory'; again, the more you have, the better.

of 256MB, and fit more if your machine will accept it (memory is relatively inexpensive).

Types of computers

There are two main types of computer in use today – PCs, which run Microsoft Windows or Linux operating systems, and Apple Macintoshes, which use their own dedicated system, known as 'OS'. The typical home computer is known as a 'desk station',

The latest iMac models from Apple Macintosh are styled very differently from traditional box-shaped computers.

whereas the smaller, briefcase-sized units are known as laptops or notebook computers. There are a variety of even smaller devices available, and as time goes by these will undoubtedly become more and more popular.

Portable computers

If you travel frequently with your camera, a laptop may be worth considering. Otherwise, there are many reasons why a desk station computer is likely to be your best choice. Faster computers are being brought out almost every day. This means that, sooner or later, your machine will need upgrading.

OPERATING SYSTEMS

An operating system is the software that a computer uses in order to function. It supervises the hardware and co-ordinates all the various programs that you run. A good, stable and fast operating system can make a computer a pleasure to use.

Computer platforms

By far the most common forms of operating systems – known as 'platforms' – are the various Microsoft Windows variants. These include Microsoft Windows 95, 98, ME, 2000 and XP. Some of these are available in different formats, such as 'Home Edition' and 'Pro'. Apple uses its own operating system for Macs known as 'OS X', which stands for 'Operating System', where the 'X' represents the version number. Unless you are an advanced user, stick with a current version.

The vast majority of personal computers across the globe run on one of the many MS Windows variants [top], but Apple Macs run their own 'OS' operating systems [bottom].

BACKING-UP YOUR WORK

An important (but often overlooked) issue when working with computers is to make sure that you have back-ups of your work, not just on your hard drive but also on a CD or DVD.

Keep your back-up disks in a secure place where they will not be damaged.

Auto saves

I have my word processor configured to save automatically every ten minutes, but in the event of a power failure the file may become corrupted, in which case you will be glad you backed it up. Additionally, if you experience a hard disk drive failure, you will be lucky to resurrect anything off it, so it is best to get into the habit of backing up.

Burning issues

A CD writer is a good investment; in fact, most new computers now come with one built in. Take the time and trouble to make CD copies of all your work, and then store them somewhere where they cannot get damaged. The process of writing a CD is known as 'burning'. Old office safes can be bought cheaply, and in the event of a fire or a break-in, your work will not be lost.

KEEPING YOUR COMPUTER VIRUS-FREE

It is a sad fact that there are a lot of malicious people who derive pleasure from creating ever more sophisticated ways of interfering with your computer from afar. The methods they use can be grouped together under the term 'viruses'. By far the most common way of viruses making their way onto your computer is through infected e-mail attachments. The amount of damage a virus can do depends on its type. Here are a few guidelines to follow if you want to keep your machine clean and unaffected.

Firewalls

One of the best ways to help reduce the ingress of unwanted programs onto your computer is to use a 'firewall'. This is a method used by a special software program to block the passage of information to and from your computer. Each time another program attempts to access your machine from the internet, the

Electronic 'firewalls' can intercept and block any unwanted programs or files, preventing them from causing harm to your computer's hard drive.

firewall intercepts it, and will only let it through if you have set the program to do so. Microsoft Windows XP has its own version of a firewall already in place.

File attachments

Never open any attachments with the file extensions 'scr', 'exe', or 'pif'. If you are in any doubt about an attached file, do not open it. Delete it from your machine immediately.

Viruses spell danger for big business, as well as for the individual computer user.

Anti-virus programs

There are a huge number of anti-virus programs available. No matter which software you use, it will only be as good as the definition files it has to work from. These files are special lists used by the anti-virus programs, which tell them what are the latest viruses and how they can be recognized. They are generally free to download, and since new viruses are coming out all the time, you can never update them often enough. Once a week is the absolute minimum if you want to stay virus-free. The best attitude to take is one of extreme caution – be complacent and your machine will become infected at some time!

MONITORS & PIXELS

When using a desk station computer, it is important that the monitor is up to the job. A poor quality screen will make all your images appear dull, lifeless, and possibly distorted.

General issues

Make sure that the monitor screen is large enough for you to work on in comfort, especially if you are doing lots of image manipulation. Monitors of superb quality have become more affordable, but good second-hand monitors can also be bought through newspaper adverts or from specialist dealers.

Consider purchasing a large, flat-screen LCD (liquid crystal display) monitor if you are going to work on lots of images on a regular basis.

How the monitor works

A desktop monitor works in much the same way as the screen in a traditional television set. However, monitors are available with many different resolutions. You can usually change the number of pixels used to make up the screen area to suit your situation as well. The higher the number of pixels used the better, although the colour setting will also influence the image quality greatly. The setting known as '16 bit High Colour' will give you good results, but '32 bit True Colour' is much better overall.

Monitor pixels

As with digital cameras, monitors compose their pictures from many thousands of pixels, each of which is controlled for colour and brightness. Controlling a grid of pixels is called 'bit mapping' and digital images are called bit maps. The higher the number of pixels, the better the resolution – and the overall picture quality. When an image is enlarged too much, it becomes possible to see the individual pixels, an undesirable effect which is known as 'pixelation'.

If you want to change or check your screen settings on a Windows-based machine, simply right-click the mouse over the desktop. When the screen appears, click the settings tab at top right, which will produce the screen shown. Select 'True Colour' – if your hardware can support it, of course.

SCANNING & RE-TOUCHING OLD IMAGES

Image editing is great for digital pictures, but it can also be used to great effect with old or damaged prints. The print first needs to be digitized. Of course, you could take a photo, but far easier would be to scan the print and save it digitally.

This is an economical flatbed scanner, suitable for home or office use.

Flatbed scanners

If you want to make a copy of a flat image, a scanner is likely to be your best option. In recent years, flatbed scanners have fallen in price to such an extent that really good ones can be obtained fairly reasonably. They are also much easier to use than their predecessors. Nowadays, all you have to do is plug them in via a USB port, load up the software CD, put the item you want to scan in place and press the 'Scan' button. The image is recorded and transferred into your graphics program, which is then automatically started for you.

When you have made a scan, the first thing to do is to resize the image using your graphics program, because it will almost certainly be at too large a size to work with.

To illustrate the type of things you can do by combining your scanner and your graphics package, here are two images (see opposite), which I recently scanned and re-touched. On top is an original page from a magazine dated 1754 entitled Smith's Newington Peach & Peacock Butterfly. You can see how the text from the facing page has stained it, and how there are various other defects on the page. On the right is the same image after I used Paint Shop Pro to re-touch it. It is worth noting that this was not a quick process, but it shows what can be done with patience and care.

With a little time and effort, you can sharpen up tired-looking prints and even change the background colour to make the page stand out.

Cleaning up

To examine in more detail how the re-touching was performed, let us take a look at a specific part of the Smith's Newington Peach & Peacock Butterfly image.

In this case the original is on the left, and we can see how badly damaged it is. In the picture below I have zoomed in by a magnification of x15 using Paint Shop

The original detail from the print is on the left, with the final retouched version on the right.

Pro on the end of the butterfly's wing. See how the image becomes a series of individual pixels at this level of magnification. It is then simply a case of going around and changing the pixel colours to those that you choose. This is done using exactly the same process as was applied earlier to re-touch the motorcycle number plate (see page 97) – that is, by using the paintbrush tool and the colour palette. If you were to do this to an image as large as this one by modifying individual pixels, the task would take forever. The trick is to use the control palette to select a large paintbrush for all the broad areas of colour, and then to keep zooming in further, using ever smaller paintbrushes until you are happy with the overall result.

There is much debate as to which is the best graphics package to use for the amateur. As with so many things in life, however, there is no single answer. The full version of Adobe Photoshop is the program most favoured by the professional. For the hobbyist user, Jasc Paint Shop Pro or Adobe Photoshop Elements are more than sufficient, unless you are after significantly more advanced features.

Other graphics programs

There are lots of other graphics programs in the marketplace and many of these are aimed at the domestic user. You may well find that they provide all the functionality you need without the complexity or expense of the larger packages. If you have access to broadband internet, then it is always worth keeping an eye on the official websites of companies such as Adobe and Jasc, since they often have time-limited trial downloads available for free.

DISPLAYING IMAGES

As well as viewing your images on your computer in thumbnail, real-size or full screen formats, it is also possible to look at them on a variety of other media.

Using 'video out' on your television

Apart from those models at the budget end of the market, most digital cameras have some form of small LCD screen on which it is possible to view your pictures. However, if you are away from your computer or have a group of people that you would like to share them with, it can be difficult trying to display them to everyone at the same time. An excellent solution to this is available if your camera has a video-out port. This will allow you to connect it to a television set through the video-in terminals. Make sure you have the correct cable – it is usually supplied with the camera.

The SanDisk Photo Viewer is ideal for domestic presentations. Using the remote, you can view, rotate and zoom into your photos on your television.

Sometimes a projector and screen will probably be a more effective means of display than a television set.

There are several useful things you can do by connecting your camera to a television. While it works well as a giant view screen, so that your family and friends can see your existing photographs, they can also

watch live images of new ones being taken. Alternatively, you can set up a video recorder and capture a whole sequence to show off later, or maybe review work you have done that day.

The Canon LV-S2 Multimedia Projector is ideal for public presentations, and for a variety of leisure or business purposes.

While a television offers an excellent way of presenting images to a small group of family and friends, it is not a very satisfactory method for presenting them to larger groups. A public display device, such as a digital projector or some sort of a cinema screen, would be ideal. For medium-sized groups of up to a hundred or so, a multimedia image projector is ideal.

Portable image storage and viewing devices

If you take a lot of photographs and like to travel light, there are several portable items of equipment

CDs or DVDs may offer a portable means of storing images, but many handheld devices can hold just as many images and also offer the facility of viewing them.

on the market to answer your needs. For example, there are handheld image storage and viewing devices available that can hold vast numbers of digital photographs – in some cases, between as many as 10,000 and 30,000!

These units can read most card formats and have sophisticated file management systems, which can store images in folders. In addition, individual files can be renamed, copied, moved around or deleted. There are also features that appeal to professional users, such as the fact that these units are able to handle images in RAW format of up to 18MB each. It is also possible to view histograms and other information, as well as to upload images from hard disk drives onto the handheld units, or to make hard copies of images by connecting directly to a printer.

Another way to view images while on the move is with a portable DVD player or a laptop computer. Since these tend to be about the same size and weight, many people cannot see the sense in paying out for a DVD player when a laptop can do so much more. There are also many

The Nixvue Vista is available in 10, 20 or 30GB capacities, and runs off lithium-ion batteries.

multimedia players on the market. These tend to have LCD screens of around 85mm (3in) in size and can play MP3 files as well as display images. Depending on the make and model, you can connect to a printer or a television. If you are considering purchasing one of these, take some time to review what each version offers – the storage capability, the types of memory cards they can accept, and so on.

The Samsung L100 DVD player is a portable unit with a screen that is similar in size to that of a laptop. However, it is rather expensive.

E-MAILING DIGITAL PHOTOS

One of the most popular ways of sharing digital photos between family and friends is by sending them by e-mail.

E-mailing issues

To send a digital photograph by e-mail is simplicity itself. However, there are a few things to watch out for. Firstly, make sure that you have shrunk the image down to a sensible size. Even if you have broadband internet access, the recipient may not, and a 15MB file on a dial-up connection will make you very unpopular indeed. A good rule of thumb is to keep the images down below 100KB.

Old technology may not be able to cope with sending and receiving large e-mail attachments, so make sure your computer hardware is up-to-date.

Blocked out

Another thing to bear in mind is to check whether your intended recipient's e-mail system will actually allow attachments through. If you are sending an e-mail to a company, many have become so security conscious that attachments are viewed with great suspicion and are often blocked out.

Which format?

It is also important to remember that not everyone has their own

Using e-mail you can send your friends and family holiday snaps from anywhere in the world.

imaging software packages, so when you send an image file by e-mail, make sure you choose the most appropriate format. If you send someone a Photoshop (.psd) or a Paintshop (.psp) file, they may well not be able to open it. JPEG and GIF files are universally accepted these days. These formats are also efficient in terms of quality and size, so they are good choices for e-mail attachments.

SENDING IMAGES BY CAMERA PHONE

Camera phones are becoming more popular. These devices are handy for commercial purposes, used by estate agents, car trader magazine staff and so on.

The Nokia 7600 Imaging Phone seen from the front [top] and rear [bottom].

It's good to snap

If you are sending a camera phone image to another camera phone, the recipient must also be on a network that can communicate with your own. A link to the photos can be sent by e-mail to anyone with an e-mail address. Recipients are sent a text message explaining how to view your photos over the internet. Your images are kept in your own personal photo album, which is protected by a password so that you can decide who gets access to your pictures. Camera phones and other devices that support this service let you include still images, video images and sounds.

SENDING IMAGES TO WEBSITES

If you are creating your own website or want to post your images onto someone else's, there are three main ways to transfer your images to the host location.

The three methods are:
- By using a file transfer program, such as FTP (this stands for 'file transfer protocol')
- By using the 'Upload' facility found on some websites
- By e-mail. This only works if you are sending them to someone else to post for you.

WS_FTP is a good example of a file transfer program. With it you can move large files from your computer to remote locations.

The best way to send large files to a website is via an FTP package. There are many different versions available, some of which can be downloaded for free from the internet. Using such a program, you can move large files from your computer across the internet to a folder at the host location. You will need to know certain technical information about the host machine. This includes the host's web address, a UserID and password.

IMAGE TYPES

Digital photography is a great medium for lots of different purposes – from holiday snaps to action at sporting events, subjects from nature and even night shots.

TAKING HOLIDAY SNAPS

Even if the photos we take on holiday do not turn out as vibrant as the scenes we remember, the digital age allows us to restore that vibrancy thanks to various image enhancements.

On location

Before the days of the digital camera, on returning from holiday we would put our films in for processing, wait at

least a few days, and then our eager anticipation would turn to disappointment as

Some holiday snaps will not need any special manipulation – they speak volumes just as they are.

we saw the results of our endeavours. However, with image manipulation software it is easy to fix problems in digital images.

Many graphics programs have an 'Enhance Photo' facility, which applies a series of enhancement operations with one click. In Paint Shop Pro this is called 'One Step Photo Fix'; in Photoshop Elements, under the 'Enhance' menu, simply click on 'Quick Fix'. If the result does not produce the desired effect, then try the manual approach by using Brightness/Contrast, then Saturation and finally Colour adjustment. All three of these operations allow

In the top image, the sign has bounced so much light back at the camera that the landscape behind it has gone very dark. In the bottom version of the image it has been possible to bring out some of the detail and colours of the background scenery.

you to tinker with the settings, so it is a good idea to play around with them (using a spare copy and not the original!), until you feel you have achieved the right combination. When you are happy with the result, you can use the sharpen tool to add crispness to your image.

On reflection

One of the big problems with taking photographs of holiday landscapes is that the difference in light levels between the sky and the ground can cause all sorts of problems. The main issue is that you can lose the blues from the sky, making the picture appear very white and bland.

This photograph of a lake in a Queensland forest suffers from a sky that is too white and scenery that is too dark. Most of this has been caused by the sky's reflection in the water, which has quite badly skewed the camera's light level calculations.

Shooting over water can exacerbate this problem, due to the reflections. Many digital cameras have an in-built bias towards the bottom of the picture to offset the effect of the sky. As soon as you get bright reflections off the water, however, the offset compensation is lost. One way around this is to take a series of photos at different aperture settings (the size that the lens opens to). Later on, when you get home and download your pictures onto your computer, you can then use your graphics package to cut the best sky out of one image and put it over the best ground from another

Once again, reflections have resulted in a loss of detail in the shadows on these fishing boats.

There are also a vast number of filters you can buy to help you take pictures without bleached sky or loss of detail. Some are more useful than others. Polarizers, for instance, are used to deepen blue skies in landscape photographs. They can also work wonders in reducing reflections when shooting through glass or water at an angle, as is the case with the examples on these pages. Neutral density filters are like sunglasses for your camera. The amount of light allowed in is reduced, but without changing the colour. Neutral density filters are often used when shooting in bright light to allow for a larger aperture and so a smaller depth of field.

PORTRAITS

A traditional portrait is of a person sitting looking straight at the camera – in my opinion, far too boring. I like to get them to use hand gestures or else add a few props around them.

Setting up the shot

You need to be careful in your choice of setting, however. If it has too many features, for instance, you can lose the main purpose of the shot. Getting the lighting right is of paramount importance – too little, and your shot will be worthless, too much and you will end up with a bleached face.

To get your subject into the right frame of mind, get them to go through a range of hand positions. No single pose will work for everyone, so take lots of shots and choose the best one.

Look for strong lines in the background, as these can ruin the effect of your portrait. Look especially for vertical objects rising out of the top of the head. Trees, the edges of buildings, window frames and all manner of other structures can create composition difficulties.

Hands-on

Most people feel nervous in front of a camera. It is entirely normal to feel this way, but it can be hard work trying to get a subject to relax, especially if you are short of time for the shot. One of the worst contributors to this

When you take portraits outdoors, bright sunlight can reflect off the face, which results in the camera miscalculating the light level settings, as here.

camera awkwardness is other people watching. Not only will the subject be nervous, but they will feel far more self-conscious, as well. If you can, it is best to clear the area, so you are left alone with your subject.

It is important that you also project a feeling of confidence. If your subject thinks that you know what you are doing and that you are going to produce good results, it is a great help in putting them at ease. One of the ways to do this is to show them the particular pose you want by mimicking it yourself.

TAKING PICTURES OF CHILDREN

Photographing children in traditional poses is generally a nightmarish prospect! Taking pictures of kids at play, on the other hand, is much easier...

Catch the moment

When it comes to taking photographs of young children, there is a whole range of issues to take into account. For a start, kids get bored very quickly, so

you cannot spend ages setting up the shots. The best thing is to be ready with the camera – kids do unexpected things at unexpected times, and you are likely to have very little time to respond.

My daughter, playing 'hide behind the tree'. Each time Carina jumped into view, she had a huge smile on her face, resulting in a series of wonderful photographs.

While large, complicated cameras will give you the best results in terms of quality, they can be very inconvenient to carry around, especially if you have to carry the child as well! It is generally better to use a smaller, aim-and-click camera so you are not hampered with camera cases and expensive lenses while chasing your subject around. Simply choose the right moment to release the shutter and there is your perfectly posed photograph!

Digital cameras are ideal to take to family events and celebrations, where they can be unobtrusively left in your pocket or handbag and whipped out when the moment arises. That way, young children are unaware

Children are often much better than adults for producing wonderfully natural smiles, which are easily captured in a photo.

that they may be thrust into the spotlight, with the danger of them turning self-conscious, and will continue just being themselves. These are the best moments to quickly take out your camera and take unposed, natural pictures, which are often far more effective than traditional group photos in which everyone stares at the camera and says 'cheese'! Above all, though, do not let photography take over your life at these events. Make sure you join in with the events you are recording!

SPORTS & PASTIMES

If you have a passion for a particular sport or pastime, then what better opportunity to share your memories than in photographs? Motor racing enthusiasts are probably the most challenged photographically – by the problems of speed.

Fast and furious

If you want to photograph fast moving objects, then practice is the best way of achieving good results. The more shots you take, the better you will get at them. Working as a racing car engineer has given me access to many areas that private individuals would never be allowed near. Some circuits have a Plexiglas safety screen in place on top of the pit wall, so even if you manage to get that close, if you were to try and take a shot through it you would get lots of reflection. Occasionally, however, you may achieve an effective blend of reflection and subject, which you can ascribe to your photographic artistry. Such pictures are often down to pure luck rather than judgement.

However, even professional photographers, especially those who specialize in motor racing, will often take hundreds of shots which end up being discarded for the one, 'spot on' image. A good example is the speeding car on the track, where practice really does make perfect.

It takes a lot of practice to get a fast moving car where you want it on frame. You need to catch the essence of speed.

With the speeds that some of these racing cars reach, it is not surprising that there is little time for focussing the shot, getting the light correct and composing the photo. Before you know it, the noise has faded into the distance and the track is again bare. Most beginners will end up with lots of shots of empty track. Usually, this is because digital cameras take some time to acquire a focus point, and the subject has passed by the time the shutter is released. To get around this, it is a good idea to get the camera focussed in on a particular section of track, and then as the car comes into the frame, release the shutter. The more times you have a go, the better the shots.

Capturing the action

Many sports and pastimes are just as fast and furious as motor racing, but require different skills with the

The zoom can bring you closer to the action and fills the frame with your subject.

camera to capture the action and excitement of specific events or fixtures. Next time you go down to the sports centre for a game of squash, cheer on your favourite football team or watch a game of cricket on the village green, make sure you take your digital camera with you. You will find a wealth of opportunities for taking action pictures at every event.

For sporting events particularly, it would be rare for you to be close up to the action. Most digital cameras offer a zoom option to get you closer to the subject, whether it be the cricketer at the crease striking the ball, a footballer at the far side of the pitch sliding in for a tackle or two fencers duelling it out in a competition. Although built-in zooms are fairly modest in comparison with the add-on professional zoom lenses you can buy, they can certainly bring you closer, filling the frame and magnifying the subject matter.

The same problems encountered with motor racing photography are also present at other fast and furious sporting events. The same principle of using faster shutter speeds to capture the fast-

You get a real feeling of action and power from this image.

moving subject is equally relevant. This can look impressive when taking shots of water sports. With a bit of practice, you can capture the drops of water held suspended in the air for a moment in time, giving the picture a sense of movement.

Capturing the people

As with most pastimes, it is the people that really matter at these events, and you can often capture a sense of excitement through the faces and

You need great timing to take good photographs of people playing sports.

expressions of the people involved, as well as the spectators. Using a tripod to ensure a completely steady shot or getting up high for an unusual overhead shot are all great devices for taking varied pictures of people and events.

Capturing the flavour

If I were to stick to just taking photographs of speeding cars in an attempt to portray what motor racing is all about to a novice, then I believe I would have failed in getting over the true flavour of the sport. A day at a racing circuit is not just about high-speed cars – as exciting as they are in their own right. The day is made up of people, events taking

All sorts of strange activities go into making up a weekend at a motor racing circuit – some of them creating great photographic opportunities!

Take some shots where there is a lot of activity going on, for added interest.

place around the circuit unrelated to motor racing, the noises and smells of gasoline and engines. A race day has real atmosphere.

Although it is impossible to capture the noise and smells in a photograph, it is possible to portray a flavour of the day's events. And this involves taking photos of the more unusual, rather than the obvious. Wander around with your camera, away from where most people think the action is taking place. (As mentioned before, though, do not miss what you have come to see!). Think about the unusual angle – get down low or else find a position high above everyone. Take a look at what people not involved in the action are doing; find the incongruous scene –

Every now and again, you will get lucky and catch someone in a pose that would be perfect for a caption contest.

Morris dancers at an outdoor rock festival, for example. Look for all the peripheral activities. For example, quad bikes towing racing tyres on a rack along the pit lane at a racing circuit. If you are trying to produce a photographic record of life at a circuit – for a magazine article, for instance – shots like these can be very useful as they give the reader more of a sense of the day; someone looking at images of varied events and activities can feel the flavour of the experience as if they had been there.

Paint it red

Every weekend, thousands of us indulge in all sorts of sports and leisure activities that involve getting dirty. Others involve putting on uniforms, such as when you take part in a paintballing session. I decided not to risk

TIP: Whenever you attend events where there are going to be lots of people and therefore lots of pushing and squeezing through crowds, you must ensure that your camera is protected and that you can keep hold of it. Your camera case therefore needs to be fairly robust to withstand the inevitable banging against people and objects.

my camera in the 'killing zone', since it was quite clear it could have been badly damaged. The safety regulations prevented us from removing our masks once out of the relaxation area anyway, and there was no way I could have taken any decent pictures with my mask still on. This is the kind of detail you need to pay attention to if you want to take photographs at many events.

My friend Rob was in his element wearing combats and paintball-shooting people! Getting people to pose in a relaxed and informal manner requires a lot of things – tact and timing being two of the most important.

NATURE PHOTOGRAPHY

The great outdoors is an excellent training ground for the amateur photographer. Not only do the seasons create varied scenes, but wildlife can present you with infinite possibilities for stunning photographs.

The natural world

Taking photographs of wildlife can be incredibly rewarding and incredibly frustrating at the same time. If you do not have a telephoto lens, you will be restricted to subjects that you can get close to. Since digital cameras with macro lenses are very expensive, let's consider what can be achieved with a mid-range compact model.

A decent mid-range digital camera is capable of taking some incredibly detailed photographs if you get everything right, as in this image of an ivy flower.

A powerful zoom allows you to photograph potentially dangerous subjects from a safe distance.

Getting down close to your subject matter is vital when photographing flora and fauna. Even with a zoom, the photographer needs to position him or herself at the correct angle. Most of the time you need to kneel down – or even lie down on your front – so that you are level with your subject. This makes the subject matter appear intimate and closer. Overhead shots are fine and produce equally satisfying results. In fact, they can sometimes give such an unusual perspective to a subject that the image becomes very striking and stands out even more. Experiment with taking photographs at different angles and different levels in relation to your subject.

Using the zoom or close-focus to home in on a single subject will make the surrounding scenery look out of focus or blurred. You can experiment with this feature, particularly in the camera's manual rather than automatic mode. The depth of field (that is, the foreground and background) will be more blurred in photos taken with a macro (close-up) feature than those taken with a zoom feature, for instance. However, you can get really close to a subject with a macro shot as opposed to a zoom. It all depends on what you are aiming at.

Butterflies

If you want an ideal subject to hone your skills on, then a suggestion is that you start with butterflies and flowers. The former will test your patience and stalking skills, while the latter will give you a chance to get some experience of sorting out the best angles and compositions.

The beautiful Comma butterfly is one of the most photogenic species. It is a relatively easy creature to capture with a camera, as it will sit and sun itself for ages.

It is a good idea to learn a little about your subjects before you go looking for them – either take an expert with you or read books about them first. It would be a real shame if you passed by the chance to photograph a rare butterfly and instead spent all your time on one of the more common species.

Flowers

Flowers can present many challenges to the photographer. For a start, they may not be in bloom for long. For example, certain tropical species may only flower for one night every few years. Others are past their best very quickly, or they may produce blooms for months on end. If you decide to enter this fascinating area of photography, start somewhere where you can set up a tripod in the

Many photographers like to produce images where the subject is in clear focus, and the background is blurred, as can be seen here. I tried enhancing this photo, but could not improve on the original image.

peace and quiet, and also preferably in a spot sheltered from the wind. For most garden flowers, begin when the sun is high in the sky. This is because many flowers will track the sun, and others will begin to close their petals around mid-afternoon. It will also allow you to site your camera and tripod with reasonable freedom – having a shadow of the photographer in the picture will not improve it!

One of the best ways to begin photographing birds is to find a local village pond with tame ducks.

Taming your subject

Animals and birds make very good subjects for nature photography. The most obvious reason for this is that, unlike people, you cannot put them in poses or situations to your liking, so your images are less likely to be overly contrived. Wild animals and birds which are nervous around human beings will be more difficult subjects to photograph than, for example, the ducks on a village pond, which may be used to people coming close to them, perhaps in order to feed them. However, you photograph wild creatures in their own environment, doing their natural thing, so the chances are that with practice you will manage to take some truly life-like images.

As with all other forms of nature photography, patience is a virtue, as is a calm approach. It is no good running about trying to round up a clutch of ducks to make up your photo composition. You may just have to wait for the right moment, as in the picture opposite, where the ducks have a complete disregard for the laws on 'parking' on double yellow lines!

Seeing the wood for the trees

Forests and woods can provide all sorts of subject matter – from the smallest fern to the mightiest of trees. If you keep a sharp eye out, there will also be animals around you, although most will sadly remain out of sight as well as out of shot, no matter how hard you search. Even if you only include plants in your image, a bit of patience and some good judgement can result in some excellent images.

The palm [right] forms a good central focal point for the composition, especially as the fallen trees conduct the eye towards it.

TAKING PICTURES FOR MAGAZINE ADVERTS

If the object you want to sell is small, then set up an area where it can be positioned under good light. If this is close to where your computer is located, then some cameras have the option of using a program called RemoteCapture.

By linking the camera with the computer, RemoteCapture gives the photographer the ability to view images from the larger format of the monitor screen, as opposed to the smaller confines of the camera's own smaller LCD screen. This one can do in

real time, while the shots are being taken. Your digital camera may not have this facility, but unless you are planning to advertise lots of objects in magazines or on

Once the shot of the object you wish to sell has been taken, you can view all sorts of image information, including a histogram and a list of all the settings used.

the web, do not worry too much. The actual principles of taking photographs for publishing purposes will be the same whether you are photographing with the RemoteCapture facility or not, for example, good lighting conditions, suitable background and well positioned objects.

Image quality is not reduced using RemoteCapture, so you can get close enough to capture some fine detail.

Using RemoteCapture

If you want to see how your sale item is likely to look on screen or in a photo advert before you take the picture, then a facility like Canon's RemoteCapture will enable you to do this. If you have a mains adapter, then you can set your camera up on a tripod and take as long as you like to get exactly the shots you want. As soon as you have taken the shots, you can check them over – on a full-size monitor screen – without leaving your chair. If the final results are not good enough, you can simply delete them and try again.

The 'Viewfinder' mode in RemoteCapture allows you to see the actual image through the camera's lens.

This means you can check that you have chosen a good angle for the shot, and whether the right amount of zoom has been used.

Taking the shots

To take the photo, with RemoteCapture running, either click on the 'Release' button in the window on screen or hit the space bar. As you take your photographs, the RemoteCapture screen keeps you well informed. At the top it tells you how many shots you have left and what quality setting you are working with, along with lots of other details.

If the item you are photographing has a shiny finish, you are likely to get flare if you use a flash [below left]. The photo on the right was also taken using a flash, but with careful positioning the flare was avoided.

If you want to advertise a car for sale, you need to strike a compromise between making the shot interesting and it being informative. And blank out the number plates...

Photographic principles

As mentioned previously, if you do not have RemoteCapture, this will not affect your ability to take studio-type photos of objects indoors – the principles are the same. However, especially regarding items for sale, do not resort to image manipulation. Buyers will soon give you bad feedback if you try to hide any damage. Lighting is very important, and if you are photographing indoors, then you may well need to use a flash. In this case, avoid 'flare' or do not use the flash at all. If it is possible, take the photos outside in natural light, taking account of the position of the sun.

PHOTOGRAPHY AT NIGHT

Taking successful images at night generally involves more time and trouble than most other forms of photography, due to the lack of natural light.

Lights out

When the sun sets, it does not mean that you have to stop taking photographs. Many wonderful shots can be captured, providing that you use a bit of imagination. Indeed, the sunset itself can be a superb subject. Silhouettes of dramatic buildings are also a favourite, as are areas of towns and cities that have been lit for public use, like sportsgrounds.

This shot of a swimming pool is so much more interesting for having been taken at night.

Judicious use of the flash can allow you to get good photographs of people – once again, it is a case of getting a lot of practice to learn the relevant lessons. Avoiding red eye is a prime example of one of the difficulties of night or low-light photography. Many digital cameras come with a built-in red eye reduction flash mode, which helps a great deal.

When the sun goes down, stunningly atmospheric shots can be taken.

All sorts of effects can be achieved at night. You might end up capturing the blur of passing cars in a town or city without meaning to, simply from applying a longer exposure on the camera to compensate for the lack of natural light. You may even produce a dramatic blurring effect of the street lights, just because you did not mount the camera on a tripod. A mistake in some people's eyes, but a stunning effect in others!

These two photos of a church are the same image. The one on the right has been enhanced using Paint Shop Pro.

DIGITAL VIDEO

While the replacement of film cameras with their digital counterparts is an issue that still raises hot debate, the same cannot be said about the ousting of analogue video by digital equipment. This is partly because video is still a relatively new phenomenon, but also because people are already used to dealing with rapid changes in the technology.

Devices like this analogue-to-digital converter will allow you to convert old video tapes quickly and easily.

WHY DIGITAL VIDEO?

Digital video recorders are still relatively expensive, as the technology they rely upon is so new. However, there are many good reasons for investing in a digital camcorder.

Advantages of digital video

There are many reasons why digital video is a 'good thing', but the most important is simply that it produces much better quality images than analogue (film) video. This is because the storage method used is a lot more efficient – it improves the sharpness and colours tremendously. Editing videos can be a thankless task, especially when there is a lot of footage to get through. Editing the old film formats required the patience of a saint,

There has been little resistance to change in the video market. This is probably because the technology has never stood still.

but digital film makes the job much simpler, and at times, fun, because the digital medium is so much easier to work with. This factor alone would justify the transition away from the analogue format, but there are lots of other benefits as well. For a start,

TIP: If you switch to digital video after using analogue tapes for any length of time, you will need to convert all your existing material into a digital form to maintain your archive.

digital camcorders are smaller and lighter as well as being able to produce much sharper images. Also, the fact that digital videos can be connected directly to a PC makes them eminently suitable for anyone who is computer literate.

Copying digital videos

Digital picture and audio quality will bring a freshness and vitality to the recordings you make that is unachievable with analogue tapes. Copying recordings is quicker and easier, too, with no resultant loss of quality.

One of the disadvantages of analogue videos is that when you copy them, the quality is degraded. Moreover, if you make a copy of a copy, you are likely to end up with very poor results indeed. With digital video, however, every copy is as good as the original, since computers can make error-free reproductions. This means that sending short video clips by e-mail or

TIP: Some digital cameras can connect directly to a VHS video recorder, meaning that you can simply play an old tape and the camera will make its own digital copy.

to websites is very easy, and when full length, high-resolution recordings are needed, it is simple to burn them onto CDs or DVDs.

Digital audio quality

Not only are digital images of a far higher quality, but so is the accompanying sound; digital camcorders can produce CD-quality audio recordings, especially when high performance microphones are used. If this is important to you, make sure that the model you are considering buying has the necessary connection sockets, or else you will have only the in-built microphone.

Manipulating video images

If you have manipulated images taken with a digital camera, you will know just what can be achieved. Ultimately, everything that you can do to a still image, you can also do to a video image, since they are basically the same thing. It is important to remember, however, that a video is comprised of 30 frames per second, so if you want to do any frame-by-frame manipulations, allow plenty of time for the project!

TYPES OF DIGITAL VIDEO CAMERA

There are a bewildering number of different digital video cameras on the market. They range from budget models for a few hundred pounds to professional units costing tens of thousands of pounds.

Given the sheer range of choice in digital video cameras, it is obviously important to decide exactly what you expect from your video camera – and how much you are prepared to pay for it – before you embark on selecting the model that is right for you.

When examining the market for a suitable model, the first thing to do is to gain an understanding of the individual features that you need to assess in order to pick the right camera. It is important to remember that, as with digital 'still' cameras, it is the quality of the optics and the resolution of the image sensor that

Several international manufacturers make camcorders aimed at the domestic user. This is the Canon MV6iMC, which is an ultra-compact multimedia camcorder that can also take still images.

dictate the maximum achievable quality of any video camera. Do not be tempted to rush in to purchasing a camera without making a proper assessment of these elements.

The Canon XL1S is a model aimed at the top of the range user.

There are four main formats available on digital camcorders:

MicroMV These camcorders record their footage as MPEG2 files – this is a high quality format with stereo audio which is the same as that used on DVDs. The tapes are very small, which helps to keep the overall size and weight of the camcorder to a minimum.

MiniDV This format produces superb images and stereo sound from very compact tapes.

Digital 8 This format uses Hi8 tapes, which makes camcorders that use them a little larger than those which use MicroMV or MiniDV tapes.

DVD-RAM Camcorders that use DVD-RAM record their footage onto reusable double-sided discs. These are smaller than regular CDs, but some can hold considerably more information – indeed, they can have up to twice the storage capacity. The format itself produces high quality outputs.

FEATURES OF DIGITAL VIDEO CAMERAS

Like ordinary digital cameras, video digital cameras generally offer a number of high-tech features designed to improve the quality of your footage.

Zoom range

There are two types of zoom range that you will see quoted for a camcorder – optical and digital. As with still image cameras, it is the figure given for the optical zoom that you should pay more attention to.

The zoom facility on a digital video camera can enable you to shoot dramatic footage like this in complete safety – well away from the action!

Weight

If you like to carry your camcorder with you a lot of the time, you may consider that its size and weight are among the most important factors when it comes to purchasing a new model.

LCD viewfinder screens allow you to use your camcorder much more easily than conventional eyepieces.

LCD viewfinder screen

If you have already used LCD viewfinder screens on digital cameras, you will know that they are much easier to use than conventional eyepiece viewfinders. For a start, you can let several people at once review footage, simply by holding the camcorder in front of them so that they can see the screen. Viewfinder screens also allow you to record scenes without making it too obvious that you are filming. Most people act differently when they know they are being watched, so it can really help you to capture natural activities by keeping the camcorder away from your eyeline. This is especially true where children are concerned. Check to see if the model you like has a colour or black and white viewfinder screen, if you have a strong preference for colour versions.

EDITING DIGITAL VIDEO

Despite the technical advantages of owning a digital video camera, what you shoot will not always be exactly what you want. However, fortunately it is easy to edit digital footage.

Once you have captured some digital video footage and downloaded it onto your computer, you are likely to want to review

This is what is known as the 'environment' in Ulead's Video Studio. In the image above, one of the sample files that comes with the package has been opened.

and edit it. You may want to add titles to your film, and maybe a music soundtrack as well, or it might be that you want to add your own commentary.

Ulead's Video Studio is a popular digital video editing program that is used by many camera users who are new to the subject. It is quick, easy and accessible and will not set you back a fortune. Another video editing program that you can use to manipulate your camcorder footage is produced by InterVideo, and is called WinProducer.

All video editing packages perform the same basic set of functions, regardless of cost. They allow you to:
• Cut and paste video scenes into a tight, cohesive sequence with smooth transitions between sections.
• Separate audio tracks for music or narration.
• Create titles that can scroll on and off screen.
• Fade your video slowly to or from black or white.
• Use built-in filters to adjust exposure or colour filming errors such as over- or under-exposure or to make minor colour corrections.

Here we see WinProducer's working environment, showing thumbnail images, a single frame from one of the clips and a series of standard movie effects.

FIREWIRE & DIGITAL VIDEO

Digital video files tend to be very big and consequently take time to download to your computer. However, data transfer technology is improving all the time.

FireWire

If you have a need to transfer large image or video files onto your computer, one of the best ways to do this is through what is known as a 'FireWire' link. Also called the i.Link by Sony and IEEE 1394 by other manufacturers, FireWire is a method of connecting two devices by a thin cable and sending high speed data between them. If you have such a capability on your camcorder, you will need to check out your computer to ensure that it has the necessary port.

One of the really useful features of FireWire is that you only need one port on your computer to accommodate the technology, as you can connect up to 63 devices in a row from only the one connection. This great advantage is made even better by the fact that you can plug and unplug these devices without having to turn the computer off – a facility called 'hot-swapping'.

As the resolution achieved by digital camcorders continues to improve, so the size of their recordings will also increase. This means that, if you are planning on using a digital camcorder, sooner or later you will need to get a FireWire card installed in your computer!

Specialist digital video

We have already looked at domestic camcorders in some detail, but at the other end of the scale are the much bigger, specialist digital television cameras and ultra high speed cameras used by

This is a professional video camera used for all manner of productions for television. It is very expensive and very heavy!

professionals. A digital television camera is a general purpose unit costing tens of thousands of pounds. It is as good at capturing racing cars out on a circuit as it is for getting in close and recording interviews. An ultra high speed camera is far more specialized, however. It can record up to 80,000 frames a second, and is used for situations in which there is a need to record very high speed events for short periods of time. Filming the movements of engine components at high revolutions is what this high-tech device was built for. It takes a highly experienced operator to get the best out of either of these cameras.

GLOSSARY

Aperture The size of the hole through which the image is focused on the sensor.
Aspect ratio The ratio of an image's height to its width.

Back-Filled This means the CCD's housing is filled with argon to prevent condensation.
Bitmap/Bmp An image format popular in the early days of PCs, but still used as the native format by the Windows operating system.
Blog This term is short for 'Web log', and is a web page or site that represents a kind of internet diary.
Bluetooth A special technical standard which allows wireless communication between devices.
Byte A unit of data equal to the amount used to represent one character.

CCD This is an image sensor; CCD stands for 'charge-coupled device'.
Clone brush This is a tool used by graphics programs to retouch images.
CMOS A sensor; CMOS stands for 'complementary metal oxide semiconductor'.
Colour depth The number of colours in an image factor. This governs the quality of your images.
CompactFlash A type of memory card used in some digital cameras.
Cropping A process used in graphics programs to cut away unwanted portions of an image.

Dialog box A window that is shown by a program that requires some kind of user input.
Digital zoom A way of magnifying an image using software techniques.
Dpi Dots per inch – it is a measure of the quality of a printed image.
Driver A piece of software that is used to make a device such as a printer work properly.
DV-format A high quality format used by some camcorders.
Dynamic range A measure of how a sensor records the bright and dark areas in a digital image.

Exposure The amount of light that is allowed to reach the image sensor which is controlled by the shutter speed and aperture setting.

Firewall A special system for keeping one or more computers safe from unwanted access.

FireWire A special method of connecting devices in which data can be transferred at high speed.

Focus The adjustment of the lens to make a subject or scene appear crisp in an image.

Format conversion A method of changing the manner in which an image is stored.

FTP Stands for 'File Transfer Protocol', and is a method of sending data across the internet.

Frame rate ...of a CCD is a measure of how fast a sensor can operate.

GIF An image format popular with website developers. It stands for 'Graphics Interchange File'.

Gigabyte (GB) A measure of the size of an amount of data, it equates to 1,000 megabytes.

Histogram This is a special chart that represents some kind of image information.

HTML code A computer code used to create some web pages.

Hyperlink a symbol on a computer screen that can be clicked to link to another location.

Incandescent A setting used to compensate for colour shifts caused by certain lighting.

Interpolation A process to improve the optical resolution of an image using software.

Iris An adjustable orifice that controls the amount of light that enters a camera.

ISO speed A number that specifies the speed of a silver-based film.

JPEG or JPG The most commonly used image format.

Kilobyte (KB) A measure of the size of an amount of data, it equates to a tenth of a megabyte.

Landscape mode A setting used for taking panoramic views of landscapes or wide objects.

LCD screens Liquid crystal displays used as viewfinders, and increasingly as monitors.

Low Sharpening A setting used to change the sharpness of an object's outline.

Macro mode A special setting for taking close-up photographs.

Megabyte A measurement of data equivalent to one million bytes.

Megapixel This refers to a CCD (or CMOS) sensor that has at least one million pixels.

Memory card A small removable data storage card used by most digital cameras.

Neutral mode The opposite of vivid mode, it records an image with no colour enhancement.

Nickel-cadmium batteries Durable rechargeable batteries for medium load use.

Nickel-metal hydride batteries Durable rechargeable batteries for high capacity use.

Optical zoom True image magnification achieved by repositioning the lenses.

Palette An array of colours or tools used in graphics programs.

Photosensitive This means that a chemical or sensor reacts to the presence of light.

Pixels The individual elements that go to make up a digital image – short for 'picture element'.

RAM Special electronic memory used by computers, it stands for 'Random Access Memory'.

RAW format A special format that uses no compression for the highest quality images.

Red eye Red eyes in images caused by the response of the human eye to electronic flashes.

Reformat A reorganization of the data storage on memory cards – it also erases all images.

Resolution A measure of the picture quality of an image – the higher the resolution the better.

SD Card A type of memory card used in some digital cameras – 'SD' stands for secure data.

Self-Timers A facility that triggers the shutter release after a set amount of time.
Shutter speed The speed at which the shutter opens and closes.
SmartMedia card A type of memory card used in some digital cameras.
Stitch mode A facility that combines a series of images into one much larger image.

Thumbnails A very small version of an image used by photo galleries and web pages.
TIFF An image format widespread in publishing – it stands for 'Tagged Image File Format'.
TTL A feature of SLR cameras, the viewfinder looks 'Through The Lens'.
Tungsten A setting used to compensate for colour shifts caused by tungsten electric lighting.

USB port A special port used to connect devices to a computer without turning it off. 'USB' stands for 'Universal Serial Bus'.
Ultra SD A type of memory card used in some digital cameras.
Ultra II CompactFlash A type of memory card used in some digital cameras.
Uninterruptible Power Supply A device used to protect a computer against power failures or surges, known as a 'UPS'.

VHS A format used for recording video films.
Viewfinder A device used to see where the camera lens is pointing – it can be optical or LCD.
Vivid mode A special camera setting used to enhance the colours of any recorded images.
Video mode A setting available on some digital cameras, it allows short video recordings.
Virus A malicious program usually sent via e-mail that can damage data or even hardware.

Wet plate collodion photography A process used by very early pioneers of photography.
White balance An adjustment made to the colours in an image to improve their accuracy.

XD card A type of memory card used in some digital cameras.

Zoom A facility that adjusts the lens to make an image seem closer.

WEBSITES & MAGAZINES

Websites for enthusiasts

A history of photography from its beginnings till the 1920s: www.rleg-gat.com/photohistory/
A site for Brownie enthusiasts:
www.members.aol.com/Chuck02178/brownie.htm
Digital Photography Review (digital photography news and reviews):
www.dpreview.com/
Megapixel (monthly digital camera web magazine):
www.megapixel.net
Outdoor Eyes (for outdoor photographers): www.outdooreyes.com/
Photo Net (discussion forums, reviews, etc.): www.photo.net/
Shortcourses: www.shortcourses.com/
The Classic Camera: http://www.cosmonet.org/camera/index_e.html

Product manufacturers' web addresses

Adobe (Photoshop and more): www.adobe.com
Canon UK's site: www.canon.co.uk/
Compaq: www.1.hp.com/
Duracell (batteries and more): www.duracell.com
Epson UK's site: www.epson.co.uk/
Fujifilm UK's site: www.fujifilm.co.uk
Gitzo (tripods and monopods, etc.): www.gitzo.com/
Gitzo's UK distributor: www.hasselblad.co.uk/
Hewlett Packard: www.hp.com/
IBM UK's site: www.ibm.com/uk/
InterVideo (WinProducer video editing software and more): www.inter-video.com
Ipswitch (FTP software): www.ipswitch.com
Jasc (Paint Shop Pro and more): www.jasc.com
Kodak: www.kodak.com
Macromedia (Dreamweaver web creation software and more):
www.macromedia.com
Microsoft (software and more): www.microsoft.com
Nero (CD burning software and other related materials):
www.ahead.de/en/index.html

Nikon UK's site: www.nikon.co.uk
Nixvue (handheld storage devices and more): www.nixvue.com
Nokia: www.nokia.com
Pacific Digital (photo frames, etc.): www.pacificdigital.com/
Powerware UK's site (uninterruptible power supplies): www.power-ware.co.uk/
Pure Digital (disposable Ritz Dakota cameras): www.puredigitalinc.com
Samsung UK's site: www.samsungelectronics.co.uk
SanDisk (memory cards, readers and more): www.sandisk.com
Sony: www.sony.com/
Ulead (Video Studio software and more): www.ulead.com

Digital photography magazines

Canadian Photo Guide (CAN)
General digital photography magazine

Digital Camera (UK)
Equipment reviews and advice

Digital Photo (UK)
Bestselling digital photography magazine. Includes projects, imaging know-how, news and reviews, as well as a companion CD

Digital Photography and Imaging (AUS)
Australia's first on-line photogaphic magazine

Digital Photography Techniques (UK)
Leading title specialising in digital photography techniques

Photo Electronic Imaging Magazine (US)
Advice on imaging technology, step-by-step downloadable tutorials, hardware and software reviews, and images from today's digital artists

Photo Life (CAN)
Canadian publication with digital photography news, a gallery, and a question and answer forum

Practical Photography (US)
General advice for people who want to improve their photographic skills

FURTHER READING

Aaland, Mikkel, & Rudolph Burger, *Digital Photography* (Random House, New York, USA 1992)

Breslow, Norman, *Basic Digital Photography* (Focal Press, London, England 1991)

Busch, David D. *Digital Photography* (MIS Press, New York, USA, 1995)

Davies, A & P Fennessy, *Digital Imaging for Photographers* (Focal Press, London, England 1998)

Farace, Joe, *Digital Imaging: Tips, Tools, and Techniques for Photographers* (Focal Press, London, England 1998)

Gardiner, Jeremy, *Digital Photo Illustration* (Van Nostrand Reinhold, New York, USA, 1994)

Glenwright, Jerry, *Digital Photography Step-by-Step* (Collins, London, England 2002)

Grotta, Sally Wiener, *Digital Imaging for Visual Artists* (Windcrest/McGraw-Hill, New York, USA, 1994)

Holzmann, Gerard J., *Beyond Photography: the Digital Darkroom* (Prentice Hall, Englewood Cliffs, USA, 1988)

IKirkland, Douglas, *Icons: Creativity With Camera & Computer* (Collins Pub., San Francisco, USA, 1993)

Larish, John J. *Digital Photography: Pictures of Tomorrow* (Micro Publishing Press, Torrance, CA, USA, 1992)

McMahan, Robert, *Pixel Photography* (Olive Press, Lake Hughes, CA, USA, 1993)

Ritchlin, Fred, *In Our Own Image: the Coming Revolution in Photography* (Aperture, New York, USA, 1990)

INDEX

ACKNOWLEDGEMENTS

The publishers wish to thank the following manufacturers for supplying images for inclusion in this book.

Ahead Software: 24(T); Apple Macintosh: 123, 124(B), 118; Canon: 16, 17(T), 112, 113, 119, 130, 135(B), 174, 175; Epson: 117; Fujifilm: 34, 46, 116; Hasselblad (UK): 44; Hewlett-Packard: 122, 134, 180; InterVideo: 179; Microsoft Corporation: 124(T); Nikon: 17(B); Nixvue: 137(T); Nokia: 140(T&B); Samsung: 137(B), 170, 171; SanDisk Corporation: 20, 22(B), 23, 24(T); Ulead: 178.

Key: T=Top; B=Bottom; L=Left; R=Right

The author would like to thank Jonathan Watts for his kind assistance and advice in compiling this book, and would like to dedicate this book to his daughters Gemma and Carina.